Dimitri D. Wittwer

The Phenomenon of Cult Brands

The Phenomenon of Cult Brands:
The Role of Culture in Building Strong Brands

Dimitri D. Wittwer

Supervising Professors:

Prof. Dr. Harley Krohmer
Institute of Marketing and Management
UNIVERSITY OF BERN
Bern, Switzerland

Prof. Dr. Keith T. Wilcox
Columbia Business School
COLUMBIA UNIVERSITY
New York City, United States

Inauguraldissertation zur Erlangung der Würde eines

DOCTOR RERUM OECONOMICARUM

der Wirtschafts- und Sozialwissenschaftlichen Fakultät der Universität Bern.

Die Fakultät hat diese Arbeit am 12. Dezember 2013 auf Antrag der
beiden Gutachter Prof. Dr. Harley Krohmer (Universität Bern) und
Prof. Dr. Keith T. Wilcox (Columbia University, New York) als Dissertation
angenommen, ohne damit zu den darin ausgesprochenen Auffassungen Stellung nehmen zu wollen.

Bibliographic information published by the Deutsche Nationalbibliothek:
Die Deutsche Nationalbibliothek lists this publication in the Deutsche Nationalbibliografie; detailed bibliographic data are available in the Internet at
http://dnb.dnb.de.

1st Edition 2014
© 2014 Dimitri Wittwer
Herstellung und Verlag:
BoD – Books on Demand, Norderstedt
ISBN 978-3-7357-9514-4

To My Family

"You can't just ask customers what they want and then try to give that to them. By the time you get it built, they'll want something new."

Steve Jobs 1989

Acknowledgment

My dissertation is a result of three and a half years of intense research conducted as a Ph.D. candidate of the Marketing Department of the University of Bern; at Columbia Business School (Columbia University, New York); and at John Molson School of Business (Concordia University, Montréal). For me these years have been not just instructive but also very inspiring.

I am very grateful to my supervisor, Prof. Dr. Harley Krohmer, who gave me the opportunity to have this valuable experience. Harley is a great scholar with an amazing conceptual skill set and a very positive attitude. It has been a privilege to have him as my mentor.

In addition to Harley, I would like to thank my co-supervisor, Keith Wilcox (Columbia University, New York) for his advice and feedback throughout the process of researching and writing my thesis. I am also very grateful to Prof. Dr. Lucia Malär (University of Bern) and Prof. Dr. Bettina Nyffenegger (University of Bern), from whom I have learned much about the process of writing a research paper. I would also like to express my gratitude to Bianca Grohmann (Concordia University, Montréal) for serving as supervisor during my period of research in Montréal and providing me with so much helpful feedback on my work.

Thanks are also extended to Prof. Dr. Heinzpeter Znoj (University of Bern), Prof. Dr. Klaus Armingeon (University of Bern), Prof. Dr. Silke Adam (University of Bern), Prof. Dr. Wayne Hoyer (University of Austin at Texas), Prof. Dr. Martin Schreier (Wirtschaftsuniversität Wien), Prof. Dr. Peter Fischer (University of St. Gallen), and Dr. Melanie Zaglia (University of Bologna)— all of whom have supported this research project through their willingness to participate either in focus groups, in-depth interviews, expert surveys, or by providing valuable feedback. Particularly, I would like to express my gratitude to David Sable (Young & Rubicam, New York), Rick Liebling (Young & Rubicam, New York), and Seth Siegel (Beanstalk, New York) for their participation in interviews. Those talks in particular have substantially increased my understanding of the cult brand phenomenon. Furthermore, I thank every single participant in my numerous online surveys and express my appreciation for the helpful comments I received from anonymous reviewers and participants in the European Marketing Association Conferences (EMAC) held in Ljubljana (2011) and in Lisbon (2012). My thanks also go out to the Uni Bern Forschungsstiftung, which generously contributed financial support to my research at Columbia University.

I also want to thank my colleagues Andreas Hediger, Andrea Kähr, Daniela Herzog, David Blatter, Olivier Pahud, and Regina Dändliker, all of whom have given me help and encouragement. Furthermore, I would like to acknowledge the help of former and current junior research assistants who have supported my work—namely, Yanick Rossier, Arrigo Cimarosti, Nicole Lymann, Elena Corazza, Lisa Schürmann, Franz Kölliker, and Martin Schopfer. Thanks also go out to students I was working with on the cult brand subject, Claudia Brodbeck, Marlène Käsermann, Terence Michel, Jéromine Siebenaler, Andrea Streiff, and Noelle Wagner. A big thank you also to Nick Crosthwaite for his great support in proofreading.

Closing on a somewhat more personal note, I want to say that I have some truly amazing friends in my life, and I will never forget that I would not be anywhere close to where I am now without each of them. Specifically, I would like to say thank you to the following people: Sibylle, for your endless support during my writing process and also for your endorsement of my long stay at Columbia University. I also thank you for making me smile every single day, thus being the most precious person in my life. Valéry, thank you for being such an inspiring and amazing brother—frankly, the best in the world. Above all, thank you, Mom and Dad! You have instilled the value of education in my mind ever since the day I was born. I am very thankful for your endless support and your habit of gently but firmly pushing me to take further steps. Without both of you, I probably wouldn't have finished even elementary school.

Dimitri D. Wittwer

Table of Contents

List of Figures

List of Tables

Abbreviations

ASC	Actual self-congruence
AVE	Average variance extracted
CBS	Cult brand status
CBSS	Cult brand status scale
CCO	Chief cultural officer
CCT	Consumer culture theory
CFA	Confirmatory factor analysis
CFI	Comparative fit index
CR	Composite reliability
EBA	Emotional brand attachment
HOG	Harley Owners Group
ISC	Ideal self-congruence
MoMA	Museum of Modern Art
NFI	Normed fit index
NNFI	Non-normed fit index
NPI	Narcissistic personality inventory
RBS	Regionalbahn Bern Solothurn
RMSEA	Root mean square error of approximation
SRMR	Standardized root mean square residual
SMC	Squared multiple correlation
WOM	Word of mouth
WTP	Willingness to pay

Introduction

When you look out into today's consumer goods-dominated world, the relevance of brands, and thus branding, is strongly apparent. There are not just new brands being launched every other day but also entirely new markets emerging. Along with this evolution, consumers increasingly do not buy products *but* brands, since they convey much more than just product features (Keller 1998). In other words, individuals buy products for what they stand for as much as for what they actually do (Levy 1959). This implies that consumers use products or brands to express desired identities (Belk 1988; Escalas and Bettman 2003). For instance, customers can use brands to display their knowledge of culture, taste, or style (Amaldoss and Jain 2005).

In this highly competitive market, billions of dollars a year are spent in the pursuit of creating strong, powerful brands. Such strong brands provide long-term growth and higher profits because they help build more loyal customers and premium prices (Chaudhuri and Holbrook 2001). It comes as no surprise that such strong brands also have higher brand values. These brand values represent only intangible value and do not include any tangible goods. Brand values can reach up to billions of dollars. For instance, Apple's brand value of $98 billion does not include office buildings and microchips. Nor does the Nescafé's brand value of more than $10 billion include its coffee plantations, machinery, or factories (Interbrand 2013). In other words, the value of a company's brand is a very important component of a company's assets and thus is of vital importance for managers. Consequently, concepts, methods, and tools that help navigate through the process of building such powerful brands are a key subject of investigation for both marketers and researchers (Aaker 1996; Keller 1998).

A key characteristic of such powerful brands is that they manage to provide particular meaning and specific, unique associations, which result in a precise brand identity. In this regard, the main challenge of building a brand is to know how to develop such a distinct brand identity. More specifically, a brand should effectively express what it stands for (Aaker 1996). By promoting clear, unique, and popular meanings, brands can inspire millions of fascinated customers. In many cases, customers of powerful brands such as Nike, Starbucks, Corona, and Ralph Lauren value these brands more for what they symbolize (i.e., brand identity) and less for the products[1] they offer. This implies that such brands deliver benefits that are not only functional in nature but also serve as more symbolic devices, conveying specific values and traits and thereby allowing customers to express themselves (Aaker 1999; Keller 1998). In other words, a brand's strong identity facilitates the expression of a customer's self.

There are some very powerful brands with very unique identities representing specific values and traits that form their ideologies. Through such strong identities, these brands succeed in building up cult-like followings, such as Red Bull (The Economist 2002), VW Beetle (Gori 2001), Harley-Davidson (Schlanger and Bhasin 2012), and Apple (Lindstrom 2011). Such brands are increasingly being described by the term *cult brand*. Managers and marketers have recognized the relevance and potential of cult brands and try to increase their brand's cult status (e.g., Brady et al. 2004; Boatwright 2013; Carr 1996; Dowling 2004; Schlanger and Bhasin 2012). However, although there is a general consensus, to the best of my knowledge there is no systematic, academic investigation of cult brands. Consequently there are no empirically founded measures to create cult brands or increase a brand's cult status.

---

[1] In the course of this dissertation, the use of the term *products* does always include services.

Against this background, I have dedicated my doctoral thesis to the examination of the phenomenon of cult brands and, at a more general level, the role of culture and cultural change in brand management. The thesis consists of three papers. While the first two papers directly relate to the focus of cult brands, the third paper deals with the examination of the role of cultural change in brand management.

In this regard, the first paper of this thesis is dedicated to the development and maintenance of cult brands as well as to the examination of the influence of cultures, subcultures, and cults in the creation and management of brands. In this first paper, I introduce the concept of culture by linking it to brands. Then I conduct qualitative research with two different perspectives in Switzerland as well as in the United States. I carried out focus-group discussions with consumers of cult brands and in-depth interviews with experts in branding and advertising. After coding the findings, putting them in a dynamic perspective enabled me to finally develop a six-stage model of how cult brands can be created. First, marketers have to analyze the predominant culture of a product category or an entire industry. This enables a marketer to gain an essential understanding of the cultural context in which the brand is supposed to be embedded. Second, I suggest the need to identify emerging cultural changes. More specifically, managers should find out if there are any societal shifts that could affect the examined culture and thus lead to a cultural change. Carrying out this step correctly is pivotal since the entire brand strategy is based upon it. In a third stage, the managers must define and concretize the brand for what it should stand for, meaning what values and meanings they want to convey. By doing so, the vanguard brand ideology, which at the same time represents the intended identity, is formulated. Fourth, the brand's ideology has to be created, at best through real stories that establish the necessary cultural-change orientation. In the fifth stage, the brand should build a fandom, devoted followers who spread the message and preach for the brand. In the sixth and last stage, marketers must establish the cultural-change orientation in brand management. This last step is crucial because it is the only way to help the brand ride out future cultural changes.

The second paper deals with the specific question of how the cult brand status can be measured. Thus, my colleagues and I developed a tool to measure cult status, resulting in the *cult brand status scale* (CBSS). This could be done only by conceptualizing cult brands on the basis of findings of the first paper and by carrying out further qualitative and quantitative research. In other words, this paper represents an expansion of the first paper. While in paper one the conceptualization was based on qualitative studies, the second paper includes an empirical, consumer-focused investigation. After we had done qualitative research, we conducted five quantitative studies in Switzerland and Canada to develop the CBSS. Our multiphase scale-development process was achieved via five studies comprising more than 5,000 study participants. It resulted in the 24-item CBSS, capable of measuring a brand's cult status via the following six dimensions: cultural-change orientation, following, pioneer, richness of story, persuasiveness, and distinctiveness. Furthermore, we linked the CBSS to theoretically and managerially relevant antecedents and outcome-variables—such as word of mouth (WOM), brand attitude, and willingness to pay (WTP)—and were able to show significant effects.

While the first and second papers directly deal with the phenomenon of cult brands, the third paper takes a somewhat different perspective on the importance of culture and cultural change in brand management. More specifically, one significant cultural change—or in other words, highly relevant societal trend—is examined: the rise of Generation Me and its impact on brand relationships and brand management. By doing so, this paper deals with the importance of cultural change in brand management. Individuals born between 1980 and 1990 express significantly higher narcissistic characteristic tendencies (Twenge 2006; Twenge and Campbell 2009). This shift can cause changing consumer attitudes toward brands and advertising. One of the objectives in this context was to examine if branding and advertising strategies for cult brands should focus on delivering either authentic or aspirational images. To that end, we tried to develop a better understanding of how the moderator variable narcissism affects the relation between actual versus ideal self-congruence on consumers' emotional brand attachment. To measure narcissistic personality traits, we used the Narcissistic Personality Inventory, or NPI-16. This framework allowed us to take the connection between the type of self-congruence (actual versus ideal self-congruence) and emotional brand attachment into consideration. By doing so, we were able to demonstrate how important cultural changes and their resulting impact can be for branding. We conducted a large-scale online study with 512 respondents and found that highly narcissistic consumers emotionally attach themselves only to actually, not ideally self-congruent cult brands. This implies that individuals of the growing narcissistic Generation Me are more attracted by real and authentic brands than by brands that offer an ideal picture. For this reason, marketers should react to such cultural changes properly and implement branding strategies that convey authentic rather than aspirational or imaginary images.

PAPER 1

Creating Cult Brands: The Cult Brand Model

For more than two decades, marketers relied on either functional or emotional branding strategies. Yet these strategies now seem to be outdated, especially since the phenomenon of cult brands has sparked the interest of brand managers and advertisers alike. Cult brands demand a different brand engagement, one that draws upon a cultural link rather than merely on product enhancements, functionality, or emotional appeal alone. In this article, I attempt to create a cult brand model that is based on widespread literature review, focus groups with consumers, and in-depth interviews with advertising and branding industry experts. Drawing upon the results of these two qualitative studies, I identify the most fundamental aspects of cult brands as being influenced by a particular cultural moment in time. Based on the interpretation of cult brands, I offer a cult brand model ranging across six stages of brand development in the following sequence: the analysis of predominant ideology; the influence of cultural change; the formulation of the vanguard brand ideology; the creation of the unique brand story; the formation of the cult following; and finally, the establishment of the cultural-change orientation. I conclude by discussing the findings in a managerial and theoretical context.

1 Introduction

In recent times, a new phenomenon to describe powerful brands has gained popularity among marketers (Atkin 2004; Brady et al. 2004; Carr 1996; Ragas and Bueno 2002). *Cult brands* such as Mini Cooper, Corona, and IKEA are highly successful because they convey special, unique identities, which help consumers express themselves and lead to a highly devoted following. Against this background, there are two main questions arising: (1) How can cult brands be created? (2) How can cult brands be managed over time? Though, prior to answering these questions, I'd like to go back one step and discuss why cult brands are more successful than other brand types. Historically, marketers and researchers believed that brands should engage the consumers by delivering indefinable emotions, such as "happiness," "fun," and "passion." The problem here is that brand attributes seem to personify abstract concepts, lacking any clear connection to the brand— and ultimately, its customer (Aaker 1999; Gobe 2001; Holt and Cameron 2010; Zaltman 2003). Often such emotional benefits become indistinguishable among brands—even across different industries or product categories. For example, who can specify the difference between SEAT's "Auto Emocion," Lee Jeans' "Live with Passion," and Lexmark's "Passion for Printing Ideas?" This means that many companies have not directly addressed this impact of culture when connecting with their customers but rather relied on branding models based on functional or emotional benefits (Aaker 2009; Keller 1993; Park, Jaworski, and MacInnis 1986). Brand managers focusing on functional or emotional benefits only, miss the most powerful aspect—cultural benefit. Today, cultural changes such as growing sustainability can, on the one hand, force the fast-food pioneer McDonald's to start stocking salad and altering its logo to a more sustainable green instead of an artificial red background for its famous golden arch (McCracken 2012;

2

Werdigier 2007). On the other hand, however, cultural changes can be the cause for strong brands such as Nokia to struggle and ultimately be pushed aside (O'Brien 2009). Such cultural changes can have significant impact on individual attitudes toward brands. Generally speaking, such changes can heavily impact consumer behavior.

Cult brands are able to attract a large number of followers since they offer them a way of expressing themselves. Some authors have gone as far as to assert that it is all about self-expression, asserting that consumers are more interested in associating themselves with a brand's identity rather than with its products. In this regard, one can think of Harley-Davidson bikers who are chiefly consuming the "freedom" associated with its brand as a lifestyle-good, which comes along with driving a Harley-Davidson (Cova and Cova 2002). As a result, brands are transformed into a symbolic resource, helping customers to construct their self-identities and lifestyles to express either who they want to be or who they actually are (Aaker 1996; Elliott 1997; Elliot and Wattanasu-wan 1998; McCracken 1987). In light of the fact that neither functional nor emotional benefits are sufficient to significantly differentiate one brand from another, it was inevitable that marketers would begin to position brands, and their products, as symbolic devices, with consumers purchasing branded prod-ucts based on their perceived broader, culture-inflected benefits (Aaker 1997; Blackston 1992; Goodyear 1993; Keller 1993). The cultural-change orientation is chiefly relevant because a culture undergoes continual changes and trans-formations (Bell 1973; Barber and Lobel 1953; Fallers 1961; Inglehart and Baker 2000; McCracken 1986). Managers must place the customers in their cultural context and create the product out of that cultural context (Holt 2004; McCracken 1987). Moreover, while interacting with customers, managers must not leave them "unconnected to a social world" or "detached from culture" (Buttle 1991, p. 97). In other words, managers must understand the cultural framework (Brooks 2013) in which they operate and communicate cultural meaning and ideology through brand stories to connect with their customers (Holt 2004). Otherwise, they are just chasing trends (McCracken 2012). For example, Steve Jobs, the cofounder of Apple, found a way to infuse aspects of culture into its products. His care for beauty, simplicity, and ease of use in an otherwise highly complex technology market helped him connect Apple to a specific subculture of the population: the creative designer, graphic artist, and photographer. Apple succeeded in promoting not only functional and emotional benefits but also, and foremost, cultural benefits. Holt (2004) argues that such symbolism goes beyond a conventional marketing approach due to its cultural and sociocultural connection (Holt 1997; 2004).

This article aims to examine the phenomenon of cult brands against a cultural context. More specifically, the primary objective is to construct a branding model that focuses on both the creation as well as the maintenance of cult brands—*the cult brand model.* The article is structured as follows: an analysis of key theories of culture and the consumer culture, including the subcultures, that can lay down the theoretical basis of this endeavor in particular. Since theory development is always exploratory in nature, I emphasize qualitative research approaches, such as focus groups and semistructured face-to-face interviews with branding and advertising experts. The final sections present the development of the cult brand model and conclude in this regard.

2 Conceptual Background

Because the comprehension of culture is pivotal to understanding cult brands, this chapter aims at putting cult in a cultural context. For this reason, I introduce in this chapter three key terms: culture, subculture, and cult, which form the conceptual background of this paper. Owing to their etymological kinship, I am able to connect cult and culture through linking subculture to both of the terms (Williams 1976).

2.1 Culture as a Basic Concept for Cult Brands

Humans differ from other species in this world because their individual identity is shaped by their culture. In simpler terms, culture is one of the most important assets of humanity. From a historical perspective, the etymological origin of the term *culture* is strongly associated with the "cultivation" of agrarian economies and religious practices. With the rise of economic development and urbanization, the Industrial Revolution brought forth a culture that was used in a religious context rather than as a synonym for "civilization." Williams (1976, p. 80) would use culture "to designate the entire way of life, activities, beliefs, and customs of a people, group, or society." Arnold (1996, p. 6) wrote that culture was "a pursuit of total perfection by means of getting to know . . . the best which has been thought and said in the world. Culture is, or ought to be, the study or pursuit of perfection." Even broader is this notion, "culture encompasses all ideas and activities with which we construe and construct our world" (McCracken 1990, p. xi). McCracken also tells us that "culture constitutes the world by supplying it with meaning" (McCracken 1986, p.72) or "the body of ideas, and activities that make up the life of a consumer" (McCracken 2012, p. 2). In keeping with Arnold's (1996) earlier conception,

Durkheim (1968) states that a society always creates an ideal that is captured by its culture.

Culture's complexity and the need to approach it cautiously are suggested by these words of Geertz (1973, p. 5): "Believing, with him [Max Weber], that man is an animal suspended in webs of significance he himself has spun, I take culture to be those webs, and the analysis of it to be therefore not an experimental science in search of law but an interpretive one in search of meaning." A culture consists of socially constructed structures of meaning; it is a symbolic system based on ideological principles (Geertz 1973). Rosman, Rubel, and Weisgrau (2009) tell us that culture is the "way of life" of a society and thus culture is closely linked to meaning and communication. People within a specific culture share specific meanings and values and have a common ground of understanding (du Gay et al. 1997). Thus culture is not simply a response to the social needs of a society but also a dynamic and motivating force (Durkheim 1968). Culture is the social legacy people adopt from the group they live in. It is a way of thinking, feeling, believing, and behaving (Kluckhohn 1994). In light of this, given the universal nature of culture, it should come as no surprise that it is the most important factor determining consumers' attitudes, behaviors, and lifestyles (Cleveland and Laroche 2007).

I have introduced a number of different interpretations of the term *culture*. For the purpose of this paper, the term *culture* will be used in a manner that expresses the way consumers' live, think, and behave in a pragmatic sense. Given our world's "freedom of thought," most of today's cultures make room for a variety of cults (Meserve 1979). In this way, it is because of an open-minded dominant culture that new cults and subcultures are able to arise. It is vitally important to remember, however, that the predominant culture— consisting of a wide range of meanings, values, attitudes, behaviors, and lifestyles—is continually being exposed to cultural change that originates in cults or subcultures. While a culture is more inclusive of a diverse set of consumer lifestyles regardless of their individual preferences, cults and subcultures only allow one specific ideology or lifestyle.

2.2   The Role of Cults and Subcultures in the Creation of Culture

The Merriam-Webster's Dictionary (2013) defines a cult as (1) "a system of religious beliefs and ritual (and its body of adherents); (2) a religion regarded as unorthodox or spurious (and its body of adherents); (3) the system of religious beliefs and practices; (4) great devotion to a person, idea, object, movement, or work (as a film or book) . . . ; (5) the object of such devotion; (6) a usually small group of people characterized by such devotion." According to this definition, a cult can either be the religion or the beliefs, the devotion itself, an object, or a group of people (devoted followers).

Subcultures, however, are cults in a cultural rather than religious context. The same dictionary defines subculture as "(1) a culture . . . derived from another culture; (2) an act or instance of producing a subculture; (3) an ethnic, regional, economic, or social group exhibiting characteristic patterns of behavior sufficient to distinguish it from others within an embracing culture of society." The dichotomy is reflected as follows: the aspect of being a specific group of people on the one hand while simultaneously holding beliefs or interests that notably deviate from the dominant culture or religion on the other.

Not just the research but also the dictionaries provide us with evidence of the overlapping characteristics of cults and subcultures. The term *cult* can be substituted for *subculture*, since a cult is "a group of people who share a common vision of the world, some withdrawing literally from society" (Appel

7

1983, p. 4). This definition is to a large extent congruent with that of subcultures—e.g., bikers, punks, and heavy-metal fans. Thorton (1997) sees a subculture as a network of meanings, styles, and lifestyle practices that are unique for this group of people. Ellwood (1987) elaborates on this relationship, or "kinship," between subcultures and cults by pointing out that a cult represents a reaction to the dominant meaning-systems in a society. However, in order to constitute such a response, the subculture must offer a solution to a particular problem or contradiction in society, just as a cult implicitly criticizes the religious establishment and offers a better alternative to it (Ellwood 1987). Thus in addition to providing certain people with a separation from the prevailing societal views, cults aim to save the world or at least to improve society by changing beliefs (Yinger 1970). Cults "are something new within an established tradition" and "involve innovation" (Collins 1991, p. 10). Cults bring something new into the predominant tradition by importing it from other societies (Collins 1991). So do subcultures, thereby providing alternative interpretations of widely held values and new ways of perceiving and approaching the social world and its shared meaning-systems (Thompson and Hytko 1997). The *subcultural-evolution model* of Bainbridge and Stark (1979) suggests that cults can lead to radical cultural changes. The emergence of a cult begins with a few individuals who have similar needs and desires; they form groups and talk about cultural disruptions (i.e., dissatisfaction with the status quo in a particular area).

The most notable quality of subcultures is their refusal to maintain the status quo behavior. In fact, subcultures define themselves through their opposition to dominant lifestyle norms, consumer identity, and mainstream consumption (Brown, Kozinets, and Sherry 2003; Kates 2002). Hebdige (1979) claims that subcultures are born in response to mainstream culture and consequently cause a change in culture or the strengthening of one. The prefix *sub* stands for a "segment of a larger culture" or a group within the larger culture or society (Hannerz 1992). According to Schouten and McAlexander (1995), subcultures are groups whose members take contrasting positions to the dominant culture. Many other writers also speak of cults as offering opposition to the dominant culture (Dawson 2006; Enroth 1979; Petersen 1982; Stark and Bainbridge 1985). For example, the movie industry defines a cult film as one in which the "subcultural ideology of the filmmaker, the film, or its audience are seen as existing in opposition to the mainstream" (Jankovich et al. 2003, p. 1).

Given that the elucidated terminologies of subcultures and cults are to a large extent congruent, I assert that traditional cults and subcultures have some common ground. Both subcultures and cults stand defiantly against the dominant culture. Both seek to subvert hierarchy—cults within a religious context and subcultures within a more sociocultural context. In other words, the emergence of cults in a religious context is similar to the emergence of a specific subculture in a consumption context. Both act as a nourishing ground for the evolution of a culture. The following Figure 1 illustrates the interplay between culture and subcultures/cults.

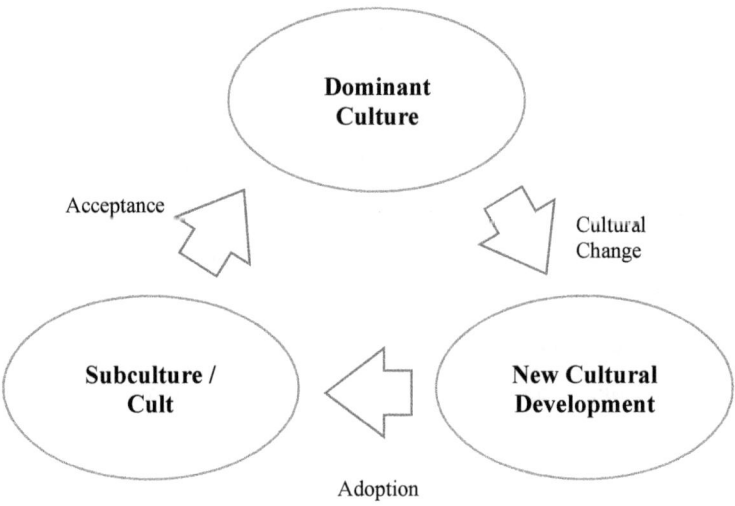

Figure 1: Interplay between Culture and Subcultures/Cults

As mentioned earlier, established cultures make room for cults or subcultures. Such dominant cultures are affected by a number of influencing factors. These changes are responsible for the emergence of new cultural developments (i.e., organic food), which in turn are being adopted by subcultures or cults (i.e., health-conscious group of people). However, once a subculture has adopted such a new cultural development, the degree of general acceptance (i.e., the mainstream) of this change is pivotal to whether it becomes a dominant culture or not.

2.3   Transferring the Concept of Sub-/Culture to a Branding Context

In developed Western societies, consumer goods play a key role. Products or product designs serve to reconstruct culture in a manner that redefines the very essence of our personal lifestyles. Can any of us imagine what our world would look like without these brands or products? Perhaps for some, but for most, culture is highly relevant to consumer goods. Many or even most of them have a significance that goes "far beyond their utilitarian aspect" (Holt 2004; Berthon et al. 2007). In this way, consumption has become a cultural phenomenon. Consumer goods have the power to convey cultural meaning (Douglas and Isherwood 1978), and thus culture and consumer goods are deeply related (McCracken 1990).

The term *consumer culture* denotes an understanding of culture in a market-oriented context (i.e., for consumer goods). It conceptualizes a system of commercial products as well as the images, videos, texts, and objects that a specific group (subculture or cult) uses to express its identity and convey its meaning (Kozinets 2001). Baudrillard (1998) sees consumer culture as a system of cultural meanings in the market. The marketplace (i.e., consumption) has become a considerable source of culture (i.e., mythic and symbolic resources), helping people to express themselves (Belk 1988). The research on consumer culture (consumer culture theory, or CCT) analyzes how historical forces such as cultural narratives, stories, myths, and ideologies affect specific manifestations of consumer culture and therefore brands (Arnould and Thompson 2005; Holt 1997; Kozinets 2002; McCracken 1990; Thompson and Hirschman 1995). Along these lines, they also focus on the cultural and sociocultural dimensions of consumption, which range from acquisition to consumption and finally to the possession of a brand (Belk, Wallendorf, and Sherry 1989; McCracken 1986). Among this range, it would seem that consumption and possession practices have been one of the most widely studied phenomena within the sphere of consumer culture (e.g., Belk, Wallendorf, and Sherry 1989; Fournier 1998; Hirschman and Holbrook 1982; Joy and Sherry 2003; Richins 1994). This suggests that we can understand consumer culture only by immersing ourselves in the many aspects of consumer symbolism: how consumers work with marketer-generated materials, lifestyle orientation, personal and collective identities, and the dynamics of sociocultural categories (Arnould and Thompson 2005; Belk, Wallendorf, and Sherry 1989; Fournier 1998; Kozinets 2001; Holt 2002).

Consumer-culture theorists also examine consumer ideology, a subject that emerges from the concept of culture. It is a system of meaning that tends to direct consumers' thoughts and actions on a cultural basis. To say that a brand or a product has an ideology is to say that it promotes a certain way of living that is defined by a particular subculture or culture (Wiedmann et al. 2011). Ideology itself has been defined in the Merriam-Webster's Dictionary as "a manner or the content of thinking characteristic of an individual, group, or culture." An ideology can encompass people's belief-systems, practices, habits, values, and customs. Values are "abstract ideals" that represent a person's "conception of the desirable" (Rokeach 1973, p. 10). Consequently an individual's beliefs, behaviors, and attitudes are explained by a person's value system (Rokeach 1973, p. 10), which in turn emerges from those cultural meanings that are so heavily promoted by products and services nowadays. Consumers use goods for cultural purposes such as to cultivate ideals, create certain lifestyles, express themselves, and gain social status (McCracken 1990). Ultimately, brands can use specific ideologies of an emerging culture and transform it into a dominant culture (Holt 2006b).

Putting the concept of culture in a branding context means studying the underlying ideological framework of consumers—what, how, and why they consume. Therefore, I claim that the cultural-change orientation of a brand is one of the most pivotal success factors for cult brands, chiefly because remarkable opportunities arise when society and its culture change. The following table provides a nonexhaustive overview of research that contributed to this cultural concept in branding, particularly for cult brands.

Author(s)	Year	Points of Conceptual Contribution	Methodology	Key Concepts
McCracken	1986	The concept and movement of cultural meaning of consumer goods. The research reveals that advertising and the fashion system can be used to transfer meaning from culture to consumer goods while consumer rituals move forth cultural meaning to the consumer.	Conceptual	Cultural meaning
McCracken	1987	The author criticizes mainly the information-based model, which is based on its nonconsideration of the consumer's cultural context but also shows deficiencies in the meaning-based model. He encourages constructing a new model that takes fuller account of a consumer's cultural context.	Conceptual	Cultural meaning
Kozinets	2001	An ethnography on the Star Trek's culture of consumption. This research suggests that to become extraordinary or even sacred, a product has to distance itself from the mainstream. It further shows that cultural and subcultural aspects are highly critical for cult brands.	Ethnography	Cult brands; cult phenomenon

Table 1: Key Literature on the Concept of Culture in Branding

Author(s)	Year	Points of Conceptual Contribution	Methodology	Key Concepts
Ragas and Bueno	2002	A practice-oriented investigation of the cult brand phenomenon. The authors present seven rules of cult branding, each referring to a number of different cult brands.	Conceptual	Cult brand
Thompson and Troester	2002	A study on the consumer value systems in the case of the natural health microculture. The authors argue that conventional theories of consumer value systems do not provide understanding enough about the cultural meaning that plays a fundamental role in consumer behavior.	Phenomenological	Cultural meaning
Holt	2002	A study of a dialectic model of branding and consumer culture focusing on the brand as an authentic cultural resource. The research shows that consumers help to reject old paradigms (i.e., ideologies) and thus create opportunities for new companies.	Interpretive study	Cultural meaning; countercultural movement

Table 1: Key Literature on the Concept of Culture in Branding (continued)

Author(s)	Year	Points of Conceptual Contribution	Methodology	Key Concepts
Holt	2004	A theory of iconic brands and cultural branding. The case-study-based research reveals that to become iconic, brands need to build on specific cultural myths and coauthor these myths.	Conceptual (case study based)	(Socio) cultural branding
Atkin	2004	An examination of (religious) cults and the application of the main characteristics to cult brands. This theoretical comparison leads to an understanding of the key characteristics of cult brands.	Conceptual	Cult brand
Kozinets and Handelman	2004	An investigation of consumer movements (i.e., sub-cultures) that try to transform the social order of consumption and marketing. These consumer movements seek ideological and cultural change.	Observational: netnograpy	Cultural change; ideology

Table 1: Key Literature on the Concept of Culture in Branding (continued)

Author(s)	Year	Points of Conceptual Contribution	Methodology	Key Concepts
Thompson and Arsel	2004	A qualitative study on the influence of global brands on a cultural system. The study illustrates how the exemplary Starbucks brand shapes cultural expectations and ideals.	Phenomenological	Cultural icon; cultural status
Twitchell	2004	An article on brands as cultural stories. The author claims that consumers desperately want meaning in their products and such meaning is rooted in mythology, folktales, or modern sagas.	Conceptual	Cult-following status; brand icon
Arnould and Thompson	2004	This article provides an overview of research on consumer culture—more specifically, on the sociocultural, experiential, symbolic, and ideological aspects of consumption. It provides four main research programs of the CCT, which are consumer identity projects, marketplace cultures, sociohistoric patterning of consumption, mass-media marketplace ideologies, and consumers' interpretive strategies.	Conceptual	Consumer culture; cultural meaning

Table 1: Key Literature on the Concept of Culture in Branding (continued)

Author(s)	Year	Points of Conceptual Contribution	Methodology	Key Concepts
Belk and Tumbat	2005	An empirical study on the extreme devotion consumers have toward specific brands and thus on their cultic consumption. The study reveals that the cult motif and the corporate mythology account for the extreme belief some customers hold in a brand.	In-depth interviewing	Brand cult
Holt	2006	An investigation of the impact of ideology on brand via a genealogical study of Jack Daniel's whiskey. His findings reveal that brands do not create new ideologies but rather benefit from already existing but often just small ideologies. They literally steal such ideologies and transform them into dominant norms.	Conceptual (case-study-based)	Iconic brands
Diamond et al.	2009	A qualitative exploration of the brand *American Girl* provides an understanding of sociocultural branding. The research reveals that the brand's creation is originated and framed by cultural themes and cultural trends.	Ethnography	(Socio) cultural branding

Table 1: Key Literature on the Concept of Culture in Branding (continued)

18

Author(s)	Year	Points of Conceptual Contribution	Methodology	Key Concepts
Schroeder	2009	A brief overview of recent research on brands as cultural, ideological, and political objects. The overview reveals that the cultural context of a brand is highly relevant for its image and the development of brand meaning.	Conceptual	Cultural codes of branding; brand culture
Holt and Cameron	2010	An advancement of Holt's (2004) *Principles of Cultural Branding*. A case-study-based model development and an application of the resultant cultural strategy model. The authors provide the genealogies of a number of brands and present a model of building cultural strategies—cultural strategy model.	Conceptual (case study based)	(Socio) cultural branding

Table 1: Key Literature on the Concept of Culture in Branding (continued)

McCracken (1986, p. 72) argues that "culture constitutes the world by supplying it with meaning." Against this background, brand meaning should be linked with culture. So cultural meaning is what a brand symbolizes to people living in a specific cultural context. It is the typical interpretation of a brand and what it stands for by people of similar values and ideologies, which are to a large extent shaped by the individual's cultural setting (Strauss and Quinn 1997). Hence, it becomes apparent that brands must deliver such cultural meaning, since they want to be perceived in a specific way by their target group. Based on this assumption, he presents a model of how cultural meaning moves from the *culturally constituted world* to the *consumer good* and finally to the *individual consumer.* He thereby stresses the relevance of goods by suggesting that they are an opportunity to create cultural meaning, which in turn allows consumers to differentiate themselves. In a related manner, McCracken (1987) discusses the information-based versus the meaning-based model of advertising. Particularly, he outlines the fact that the information-based model ignores the crucial fact that consumers are embedded in a cultural context. This oversight of the cultural context is wrong since every individual is a member of a culture and thus sees the world through a cultural lens. In addition, Kozinets (2001) picks up on the relevance of cultural and subcultural meaning of cult products. He argues that marketers must consider the cultural and subcultural context when creating brands. Thompson and Troester (2002) tie in with the growing recognition that cultural meanings play a crucial role between values—ideology—and specific attitudes and behaviors of consumers. In other words, consumers are surrounded by the culture in which their ideologies are formed. Specific products or brands must deliver specific cultural meaning to fit the consumers' values and attitudes—with their ideology. This assertion has also been proven by Kozinets and Handelman's (2004) investigation of consumer movements. Building from a basis in the New Social Movement theory, the authors suggest that there are groups of people who want to transform consumer culture and ideology. The findings of their investigation show that the ideologies of such groups are in line with the ideologies in social movements (Touraine 1981), consisting of three elements: identity, opposition, and totality. This article draws parallels to the relevance of subcultures in the creation of cult brands, as they, too, try to change the way of thinking of the mainstream.

In a similar vein, Thompson and Arsel (2004) illustrate how large brands such as Microsoft, Starbucks, Nike, and McDonald's are exposed to countercultural movements. Such movements originate in subcultures and incorporate a specific ideology resulting out of cultural changes. Against the background of emerging countercultural movements, Holt (2002) examines how branding and consumer culture evolve. One main point in this regard is that brands have to contribute as a cultural resource. In other words, brands will have to contribute to the consumers' identity projects by providing a distinct ideology consisting of cultural meaning. In keeping with these explanations, Holt (2006a) reasserts that brand plays a key ideological role for consumers. He argues that brands pick up on strong ideological currents in society, rather than creating them. The necessity of expressing cultural meaning for brands is also shown in Diamond et al. (2009). The authors posit that a brand's creation is initiated and framed by cultural themes that in turn give meaning to the brand. In his book, Holt (2004) introduces a culture-based multistep model of how brands can *become iconic*. He defines iconic brands as "an identity brand that approaches the identity value of a cultural icon" (Holt 2004, p. 11). Additionally, Schroeder (2009) sees brands as ideological referents that construct cultural meaning and social norms. It becomes apparent that the cultural meaning of iconic brands is similar to that of cult brands. In the book Holt authored with Cameron (2010), they advance the idea of cultural branding, presenting the cultural innovation theory as well as the cultural strategy model.

Against this background, Holt has clearly influenced my way of think-ing to a large extent. Although the cultural link of iconic brands is also highly relevant for cult brands, the concepts are not congruent. Therefore, I want to go beyond this for three reasons: First, descriptive characteristics of cult brands other than that of the cultural link are not covered by the concept of iconic brands. Thus, my objective is to find the main characteristics of a cult brand and determine how—if at all—through a particular branding model a cult brand can be created. Second, Holt (2004) as well as Holt and Cameron (2010) look at brands through the lens of mythmaking, whereas I take the position that the creation of cult brands is not based solely on myths but on actual cultural meaning conveyed through *true* stories and happenings—after all, a myth is "an idea or story that is believed by many people but that is *not* true" (Merri-am-Webster's Dictionary 2013). Third, and to the best of my knowledge, Holt and Cameron (2010) base their work mainly on case studies and personal expe-rience. In contrast, I draw on empirical research in this regard, both qualitative and quantitative. In addition, I claim that cult status very often is a preliminary phase for iconicity. In other words, some strong cult brands possibly achieve iconic status after a long period of time.

Another important aspect when it comes to the context of culture is the vital importance of brand stories. Twitchell (2004, p. 487) argues that individ-uals believe in stories or brand sagas because they "desperately want mean-ing." Brand stories as well as myths are able to convey cultural meaning and are helpful in building up cult-communities. By investigating *brand cult,* Belk and Tumbat (2005) identify mainly myths to be central factors for consumers' extreme devotion toward a brand, such as Apple. In addition, Atkin (2004) examines the consumers' devotion by providing a theoretical definition of cult brands. His definition outlines four major aspects of cult brands: the great exclusive devotion, the distinct ideology, the well-defined community, and the voluntary advocates. Another practical perspective is offered by Ragas and Bueno (2002), who bring up seven rules of cult branding that are merely based on a religious background.

The key literature has illustrated four concepts, that contribute to the understanding of culture in the context of branding: cultural meaning, consumer movements, cult following, and (socio) cultural branding. While some of these concepts address more directly the phenomenon of cult brands, others lay down the more abstract phenomenon of cultural branding. However, there is missing a clear empirically founded derivation of what cult brands are and how they can be created. Against this background, I choose an explorative research approach focusing on qualitative interviews, to close this research gap and to, first, find out what characterizes a cult brand and, second, how such cult brands can be created.

3   Qualitative Analysis and Measurement

The studies reported here were designed to evoke interpretations of cult brands from consumers as well as marketing experts. As such, I decided to conduct a dyadic research, in a first step, seeking to deduce the most descriptive characteristics of a cult brand in the perception of consumers. In my second step, I analyzed whether the consumer's view of cult brands is shared by branding and advertising experts, including how such a model could be developed to build the brand itself. Because my investigation is exploratory, and since its main objective is to develop a grounded model of cult branding, I have followed the guidelines for grounded theory development (Deshpandé 1983; Glaser and Strauss 1967). I collected data from both consumers and experts. This approach demands a constant comparison of the data throughout the process of data collection and analysis. In contrast to conventional hypothetico-deductive approaches where a specific theory is underlying, this research method allows patterns to emerge. These patterns provided the basis for the model to be developed. In the course of data collection, I sorted and noted those concurring statements of participants that supported the evolving categories (Isabella 1990). After the data collection, the statements were examined to see if they fitted into one of the evolved categories. By analyzing the comments of both consumers and experts, I was able to gain some elementary insights into what a cult brand is, what it relies upon, what its characteristics are, and most importantly what the secret behind it is, and was thereby able to construct the cult brand model.

In the first of the two studies, I examined the general public's understanding of the cult brand phenomenon by conducting focus-group discussions with consumers. In the second study, I sought to take a more practical view of my findings by carrying out in-depth interviews with branding and advertising experts. Based on the preceding literature review and the two studies, I developed the cult brand model that is presented in section five.

3.1 Study 1, Consumer Perspective: Focus-Group Discussion

In the first study, focus groups were assembled to elicit as much information as possible about the participants' relationships to cult brands and potential cult brands (Wilkinson 2003). Participants were asked questions such as how they perceive cult brands; how they would describe them, including any important characteristics; and how and why a brand attains cult status.

3.1.1 Sample, Procedure, and Measures

Four separate focus-group discussions with 18 participants were set up, all of whom are customers of such brands as Apple (2 participants), Converse (1), easyJet (1), Facebook (1), Ferrari (1), Fiat 500 (1), Harley-Davidson (1), IKEA (1), Le Corbusier (1), Migros (1), Nike (2), Red Bull (1), Starbucks (2), The Simpsons (1), and Vespa (1). These customers are those with expertise about their respective brands. Each discussion lasted for between one and a half to two hours. The participants' ages ranged from 23 to 52, a range that allowed the analysis to capture any age-related difference in the understanding of cult brands (44.4% female, median age = 32 years). All of the focus-group discussions took place during the week of September 22, 2010. These discussions were audiotaped, subsequently analyzed multiple times based on the transcripts and recordings, and coded, so as to capture as many relevant characteristics of cult brands as possible (Calder 1977; Fern 1982; Miles and Huberman 1994).

3.1.2 Results

The content analysis revealed that all of the statements made during the four focus-group discussions fell into one of five major subject areas. There was considerable recognition that explicit cultural meaning is the basis of a cult brand. Although cultural change was cited as being the foremost component, four other characteristics were also linked by the participants to cult brands. All characteristics serve as the ensuing subheadings.

Cultural Origin

The key finding as a result of this study is that to a very large extent, a cult brand draws upon culture. However, this link to culture can be of lower or higher intensity and can be expressed through myriad aspects. In keeping with the understanding of a cult brand's sociocultural nature as discussed in the literature is this statement made by a Harley-Davidson customer: "A cult brand has its roots somewhere in society. The best cult brands originate when needs in society shift and new opportunities emerge. A cult brand thus is a cultural and societal phenomenon." The key point was that most participants placed significant value on the fact that culture is imbued into a cult brand. In addition, among all participants, the link to culture is pivotal to its cult status. While prior studies have already mentioned the importance of cultural origin in brand management (Holt 2000; McCracken 1986), this study expands this view to cult brands.

In many other cases, the cultural aspects of cult brands stem from a kind of countercultural movement. For example, an interesting point was made in this regard by a Red Bull customer. She began by noting that "Pepsi-Cola has cult status only because it's the movement against Coca-Cola—the anti-Coke." She then went on to say, "A cult brand in the beginning is supposed to have a clear statement which contradicts another belief—in many cases a mainstream one." Simply put, a cult brand implicitly or explicitly calls into question a cultural viewpoint or social custom. A good example of this is the TV show *The Simpsons*. A Simpsons fan said, "I just love the show, because it mirrors the society we live in. And it questions the values and the culture of Western society in such a fun but true way." This implies that a cult brand arises in a subculture that stands somewhat apart from mainstream values and contradicts the dominant culture. This is in line with Kozinets and Handelman's (2004) theory of consumer movements, derived from the new social movement theory. Such consumer movements intend to change the social order and through novel ideologies try to radicalize the mainstream views.

As we have seen, subcultures or cults arise out of cultural change. In addition, a Nike customer noted that "every cult brand originates on the periphery. Nike's fight against racism had a sort of peripheral beginning, as no other brand back then was addressing social issues like this." A Fiat 500 owner suggested that "to become a cult brand there must be a group of people that is contrary to the established cultural setting; more precisely, some sort of movement against the mainstream." Such sociocultural movements try to influence and even change the surrounding culture by offering alternative ideologies embodied in products or services. Thus, a consumer movement can arise out of a subculture caused by a cultural change. The most basic point here is that there is often a connection between a cult brand and the culture out of which it emerged. This aspect is shared by Kozinets (2001), who sees the cult movie *Star Trek* as a cultural phenomenon. Furthermore, a social movement starts in a smaller group but grows and is made famous by many people. Also, a cult brand first emerges in a particular subculture and then slowly or quickly gains attractiveness, which enables it to affiliate itself with the broader and bigger culture. "Even if we all accept Apple as being a cult brand, there's a movement based on Android operating systems happening already," an Apple customer claimed. This example could not be more pertinent. Android is a countercultural movement, as evidenced by their refusal to be controlled by Apple, instead offering something new that allows everyone to upload new applications—a situation similar to that of Linux, when Microsoft was taking off.

Vanguard Brand Ideology

A scholar of politics brought us back to the essential subculture point as he noted that "cult brands in any case develop something which is seen as undoubtedly great by a specific group." When, however, is a brand just a *popular* trend rather than a true *cult* brand? Certainly there are brands that pick up on a fad and ride its popularity for a certain time. These are not cult brands, though, because they arose in the mainstream culture instead of in a subculture. Additionally, such brands aren't based on culture. Such merely trendy or popular brands tend to lack innovation and creativity as they rarely contribute any significant product advancement for the industry. For example, a Converse fan commented that "a cult brand does not join a trend but rather sets a new trend. Cult brands do not simply follow any other fad but truly create new paths themselves." As accurate as that point may be, it also is true that trends are important even for well-established cult brands because they have to respond to them if they want "to stay on the ball." In another example, a Ferrari fan, who also is a sports marketing scholar confirms this point by commenting that "Ferrari definitely is a cult brand, but they still have had to at least partially adapt themselves to trends, such as the ecological aspects of their industry, for example mileage." Against this background, it makes sense that a cult brand takes on a vanguard role in its specific product category. "To me one of the most important aspects of cult brands is the idea of being a pioneer in a specific product category," a focus-group participant and IKEA customer stated. "Let's think of IKEA, revolutionizing the furniture industry, as a pioneer," she added. That low-budget furniture retailer, known for its modern architectural design and its innovative and ready-to-assemble products, opened its first store in Switzerland in the early 1970s. We noted earlier that cults and subcultures carry a novel ideology but in fact this ideology is, not only novel, but truly innovative and thus vanguard. This vanguard aspect may not necessarily concern the innovativeness of just the product itself (i.e., the core idea) but also the way the brand appears within the market (e.g., packaging, advertising, communication). Apparently this vanguard aspect stems from the fact that a unique cultural context causes the brand to stand out conspicuously from the competition. Through such a vanguard brand ideology, cult brands stand out in their product category, providing specific meaning and values. This meaning and value (i.e., ideology) enables the consumers to express themselves (Hirschman 1983).

Another example that a number of participants cited is Harley-Davidson, which was one of the first brands to conspicuously connect a bike ride with lifestyle. The consensus that emerged here was that cult brands tend to be first movers, when it comes not just to their core product but also to surrounding endeavors. A physician and Migros customer tells the company's story: "Migros Budget, the low-cost product line of the Swiss retailer Migros, launched somewhat before 2000, I think. Swiss people had never seen anything similar to this brand. While there already were low-cost grocery retailers in Switzerland, Migros pioneered by being innovative, combining its brand that stands for quality but at a low cost." Yet another vanguard notion was mentioned in the context of low-cost airlines. For example, an easyJet customer commented, "The world is getting more connected and nowadays people want to travel more than they used to. Ryanair and easyJet noticed this change and introduced to Europe the innovative low-cost airline model of the U.S.-based Southwest Airlines. This vanguard approach of the two airlines, based on the sociocultural change, literally turned the entire European airline industry upside down." Clearly, the pioneering approach is never more potently associated with a cult brand than in the case of a cultural change.

Unique Brand Story

Another finding of this study is the narrative nature of cult brands. A fan of Le Corbusier explained that "a cult stems from the Latin *cultus*. It is, however, a past participle, and thus means something that has *already* been cultivated." He went on to elucidate the term *status* which again is a past participle, this time of *stare,* meaning to stand. The point is that something has to move, or more broadly to grow, to reach a final status. A Vespa customer concurred by saying that "indeed, a cult brand is characterized by its great, rich story." Another participant brought that assertion into question when she said this: "There's no doubt Facebook is a cult brand. I mean it has just brought a completely new approach to our social behavior, and how we interact with each other. However, Facebook's story goes back only a couple of years, so there almost is no story." This raises the obvious questions of the length of time needed to create a credible story. Is ten years enough? In the case of information technology, a very fast-changing and developing discipline, the answer seems to be yes, whereas Harley-Davidson's story has to go back at least a couple of decades. A Ferrari fan claimed, "No, a cult brand has to be known over generations. Otherwise it's not a clear cult brand." Other participants argued that time can help a cult brand when it comes to identity formation; older brands have a more authentic story than younger brands. Nonetheless, one of the participants went on to note that "technically an older brand is more likely to achieve cult status, but to me time can't constitute a cult brand; there are other much more important characteristics." This discussion draws parallels to the concept of *retro brand* (Brown, Kozinets, and Sherry 2003) and the relevance of meaning-filled narratives based on the brand's past.

That statement seems quite comprehensible, since there are many brands with long stories but no cult status. Citibank, Gant, and Tag Heuer, for instance, are not cult brands primarily because they did not arise out of a cultural change and their story does not rely on any particular cultural connection. Gant goes back to the fifties; ever since then Gant has designed, produced, and sold textile and apparel products. Some fashion labels do, in fact, produce culture, but not all products have come in response to a cultural change; that's why they cannot be cult brands. However, a Facebook user found some common ground for us to stand on: "A cult brand with some sort of cultural story is just stronger than one without." That point was confirmed, in a way, by a Fiat 500 owner who explained, "The new Fiat Cinquecento, launched in 2007, is based on the cult car launched back in 1957. Because of that, the new Cinquecento most likely will achieve cult status too." The key distinction seems to be that a cult brand must have a cultural story to tell, rather than just a long story going back multiple decades or even centuries. This discussion is also widely supported by the consumer culture theory (CCT; Arnould and Thompson 2005), where a brand's historical force (e.g., cultural narrative, myth, and ideologies) has remarkable relevance.

Cult Following

There is a logical connection between society and cult brands. An Apple en-
thusiast asserted that "at the beginning it only needs a certain group of people
behind a product to make it a cult product; however, both the product and the
group must be capable of convincing others of what they believe and thus
make the following grow." He added "I mean, cult is intertwined with mainstream; a product only reaches cult status when it attracts more than just a few
early followers. For a brand to be a cult brand, [it] must attract people like you
and me. It must be able to attract more than just its early few followers." The
important issue here is that the early following, consisting of a few people, has
to convince a sufficient number of others, if the cult brand is to move into the
mainstream and become a dominant culture. However, it is likely for cult
brands to attract a large number of followers since they have a strong identity.
A Vespa owner put it this way: "Cult brands have such a powerful expression
that makes it easy for them to attract loads of people." He further stated,
"When I mount my Vespa, I can literally feel the Italian way of life." Another
participant said that "there are certain kinds of groups that identify themselves
with specific products, music, or clothes, and they only can do that because of
the very explicit position of the brand." "A cult brand," she further stated,
"stands for a specific lifestyle that matches with that of its customers." These
values are represented by the brand identity, which in turn is the basis for the
establishment of a strong bond between individuals and the brand. These
quotes are inline with how Acosta and Devasagayam (2010, p. 165) put it,
referring to Belk and Sherry (2007): "A brand is often perceived as an exten-
sion of one's own self, a reflection of who one is as a person." Strong and
well-known brands such as Mars, Samsung, Swiss Air Lines, and HSBC also
have their loyal customers or even communities. A cult brand's following,

however, is much more intense. As an Apple fan noted, "The followers of—say, Apple—literally celebrate their purchase or feel proud when they use it." She further noted that "consumers of a particular product define themselves by consuming it and thus feel part of the community."

Another issue that came up in the course of discussion is the subject of reference that judges one brand to be a cult brand and another not to be. In other words, who can determine that Harley-Davidson is in fact a cult brand? One participant persuasively argued, "cult brands are a societal rather than an individual construct. I can consider a brand a cult brand for several reasons, without being emotionally attached to it. For example: Even if I wanted to blow up the headquarters of Pepsi-Cola (a brand that I do not like), I would still have to admit it's a cult brand—objectively. I guess it's because I know that there is a large following for this brand out there; I just have to admit it." It seems, then, that it is society that decides whether a brand is or is not a cult brand; neither a specific fandom nor a specific group of experts gets the last word.

Persistence

According to another participant, a sports brand manager, cult brands first target a small group of people (i.e., subculture) instead of the mass population. While that may be the case, the fact remains that at that early point in time, they cannot yet safely be considered cult brands. This reference to time reminds us of the need to gain a dynamic perspective on cult brands. According to a Starbucks fan, a cult that expresses specific values is inevitably related to charismatic personalities such as Gandhi, Mother Theresa, and Blocher. He went on to suggest that "cult brands always stand for something, define something. Such charisma can wear out over time, but a cult brand, same as a cult person always remains cult." However, a cult brand being in the mass market may weaken the connection to the subculture and thus ultimately undermine a cult brand's status. In contrast, a Starbucks customer argued, "It might be difficult for a brand to keep its cult status once it has been consumed by the masses." With regard to these contrary statements, a cult brand's meaning may vary over time or even decrease, but it keeps its cult status. The fact that brand meanings can vary over time has also been discussed in literature, such as Berthone et al.'s (2007). The current study expands the thinking in this area by transferring that idea to a cult brand context. It is an important issue here because it might weaken the cult brand status.

3.2 Study 2, Expert Perspective: In-Depth Interviews

This study was conducted to find out (a) what constitutes a cult brand from the perspective of an expert; and (b) whether the five main subjects of Study 1 are supported. Furthermore, I wanted to gain information on how such cult brands can be created.

3.2.1 Sample, Procedure, and Measures

In a second step, I relied on expert input to collect further insights. I contacted 23 carefully selected individuals employed by eight different advertising agencies or branding companies located in New York City or Zurich.[2] I described the focus of the study, asked for an interview, and offered a copy of the research findings as an incentive for participation. In-depth interviews were

---

[2] Some of the interviews in Zurich have been carried out in cooperation with my student, Claudia Brodbeck.

conducted as a data collection method. I asked the experts questions about what cult brands are, what their main characteristics are, how they can be developed, to what extent culture is relevant to cult brands, and what is crucial when creating them. This research method helps to gain insights into the respondents' own interpretations of their environment. In-depth interviews also enhance the researcher's ability to understand underlying questions (Miles and Huberman 1994). I conducted seven semistructured interviews with people occupying such positions as creative director, creative culturalist, strategy director, chief executive director, and branding consultant. These people work, among others, for renowned marketing and communication companies such as Beanstalk, Leo Burnett, Wunderman, and Young & Rubicam. The participants' ages ranged from 36 to 58. Six of the interviewees were male, and one was female. All of the interviews took place during the months of June, July, and August 2013. The interviews were audiotaped, analyzed multiple times, and coded (Calder 1977; Fern 1982; Miles and Huberman 1994), so as to identify all relevant characteristics of cult brands.

3.2.2 Results

The main theme to emerge from the focus groups in Study 1 was the idea that a cult brand arises out of a cultural change. The understanding I gained of this dimension is very much in line with the findings of the experts I interviewed. They pointed to cultural change as by far the most crucial instigator of cult brands. This study also showed consistent support for vanguard brand ideology, unique brand story, cult following, and persistence.

Cultural Origin

Along with customers, experts take the view that brands can achieve cult status only by being strongly attached to culture. A senior branding consultant pointed out, "A cult brand is a cultural product of the zeitgeist and it's fully aligned with a specific cultural happening. This is why it's so compelling." The zeitgeist, in this context, can mean to adapt to changes in culture—the cultural meaning. A chief executive officer even claimed, "A cult brand, to me, is when a brand moves from its main field of operation into another field of culture, such as music, theater, arts, or fashion." An excellent example of that process is provided by the current (June through September 2013) exhibition on the work of Le Corbusier at the Museum of Modern Art in New York. MoMA is displaying the LC4 chair in an exhibition. According to the interviewee, "This makes Le Corbusier and at the same time the LC4 chair a cult brand." Thus we see yet again that a cult brand does arise from culture. The strength of this "culture connection" is implicitly confirmed by the words of a creative director that noted, "There are numerous cultural productions, such as theaters, movies, and fashion shows, where Harley-Davidson bikes are used. However, a Suzuki motorcycle I've never come across, in a similar relation, and that's what makes a brand a cult brand."

Along with the focus groups, the experts also pointed out the relevance of subcultures to cult brands, noting that a cult brand always starts in a specific subculture and then grows and causes a cultural change. A chief executive officer of an advertising agency noted, "A cult brand is a brand that begins with a small, passionate group of people who fervently believe in that brand." He then added, "This brand has a special meaning to them." We saw earlier that cultural meaning is a crucial characteristic of cult brands. This particular CEO alluded to Converse being seen as a cult brand when he was growing up owing to the many passionate basketball players in city parks who wore Converse. "To play basketball back then, you had to wear Converse," he laughed.

Here is what a creative director had to say on the same subject: "Cult brands simply anticipate cultural changes and offer products based on a new belief-system—different from the dominant one." As such a cult brand grows and comes close to becoming an accepted religion; it may even overtake and replace the predominant religion (Collins 1991).

Another point in this matter was made by a creative culturalist, saying that "probably a lot of cult brands have a defining figure who leads them, who is true to his vision, such as Steve Jobs at Apple, Phil Knight at Nike, and Howard Schultz at Starbucks. These strong figures 'say no, we're not going to go after that larger, easier market and list our products in Walmart.' Instead they stick to their original plan and intentionally decide to grow slower." Thus, cult brands keep with their customers' beliefs of the brand, its ideology. A very similar aspect has been found in the literature. Atkin (2004) points out that cult brands have beliefs and morals and embody values. They have a clear vision and stand up for things, he argues.

Vanguard Brand Ideology

A creative culturalist put this another way, in the context of creating cult brands: "What one should do is look at a market and find out the rules for this industry and then flip it up." This statement clearly indicates a pronounced characteristic of a cult, its ability to create novel belief systems. As I have mentioned earlier in this article, cults create novel belief systems. A strategy director noted, "Southwest Airlines made flying a different experience at a much cheaper price." They dramatically impacted the airline industry, creating a completely new corporate culture and introducing the low-price flights that now account for an entire submarket within the airline industry. He went on to state, "Or take Cirque du Soleil. They knew the predominant culture in the circus industry. They knew that this is how it 'has to be.' These are everyone's expectations. But they decided to launch a totally novel and different circus from what people knew of then." To be a pioneer in a specific product category is critical to gain cult brand status. This is confirmed by Atkin (2004, p. 17) when he noted that "cult brands need to separate themselves from the status quo." A creative director reasserted, "I guess cult brands think outside the box, and in any case bring something totally new into the marketplace. I don't mean that only with regard to the product but also to the way they communicate, what measures they employ, what design they choose, or how their customer service is built. Cult brands bring a new way of thinking, a new lifestyle into a marketplace. I guess that's why they're cult brands."

A chief creative officer noted, "A cult brand emerges from a 'pull linkage' in society, where something new, in particular new value systems, can arise." This particular statement is to a large extent congruent with what Holt (2004) identified as main characteristic of an iconic brand. Nonetheless, these new value systems are little accepted in the beginning of a cult brand. For that reason, cult brands often portray an "us versus the world" mentality. In this way, they demarcate themselves from their competitors. Apparently a cult brand's values and beliefs are indeed deviant and novel so that they contradict mainstream beliefs. In fact, because they want to bring in a new ideology, they are different and want to be perceived as different. A strategy director goes on to reiterate, "What sets cult brands apart is that they don't try to please everybody. Their specific values, lifestyles actively exclude certain people." This is indeed an interesting point, as Red Bull is very clearly saying that they are not for everybody. Another aspect that emerged from the interviews is that cult brands do not take the least-common-denominator approach to their brand or their marketing. They want to be unique. For example, a creative director mentioned, "They [cult brands] are saying to some degree that they are taking some flak for who they are, what they stand for, and what they believe in." This implies another point. He goes on to say that "they are not only saying 'this is what we are, but also this is what we're not.' This makes certain people say, 'Ah yes, that brand understands me! I do like that brand, and I don't like that other thing.'" Specific, unique ideologies attract consumers because they want to differentiate themselves from others (Snyder and Fromkin 1980). Individuals have a desire to express specific identities rather than common ones (Berger and Heath 2007), and cult brands offer such specific identities by providing unique ideologies.

Unique Brand Story

In the course of many of the interviews I carried out, I noticed that a cult brand's story is another crucial feature. A strategy director argued, "Well, if you look at cult brands—say, Apple, Starbucks, or Corona—their common ground is the strong story they actively tell. But seriously, it's not a random story but a story that connects the cult brand's ideology with the brand. In many cases I would argue the story is indeed based on facts." Another interviewee, a senior account manager, supported this statement, saying, "It's not that noncult brands cannot have a strong story either. They absolutely can. Listen, I think noncult brands, if they have a good story, they simply don't tell it how cult brands do. They just don't take advantage of that great opportunity they could have." A strategy director pointed out that cult brands employ storytelling as no other brand does, saying, "Cult brands really know how to cope with conveying their values and beliefs by means of the story they tell. They literally instill their values and beliefs in their customers' minds." So cult brands do not simply tell a compelling story as many successful brands do: they portray a story that connects the ideology of the subculture (and culture) with the brand. Patterson and Brown (2005) suggests that the most compelling brands tell strong stories that are built on other stories of the brand.

Another interesting viewpoint emerged from a chief executive officer's statement: "People don't buy what you do, but why you do it!" So the actual ideology—or in other words, the meaning of a brand, its lifestyle, and way of thinking—is much more important than the product itself. This statement is perfectly reinforced by the literature on cultural meaning, first and foremost McCracken's (1986). This supports the brand story theory, because it is through its story that a brand can best convey its ideology. The pivotal importance of storytelling in successfully communicating messages and engaging people has also been shown in managerial literature, such as McKee's (2003), and in the field of psychology (Woodside, Sood, and Miller 2008).

Cult Following

A further aspect of cult brands that emerged during the interviews is their availability. A chief executive officer remembered that in the not-so-distant past, "you had to go look to find Converse. They weren't available just everywhere." He pointed out that "a cult brand by definition has to be harder to find. I also think the cult brands are all made up by word of mouth. You knew about it and its story because somebody wore it. Somebody told you about it." This implies that once you get a pair of Converse, you become more attached to the brand and are proud to own them. Similarly, a content director reminds us, "Apple can predict the exact amount of iPhones they will be selling when they launch a new one. But they shorten the supply on purpose, to have customers, chiefly devoted followers, spending the night in front of the stores before its launch." This could also have a signaling effect on potential customers, making them believe that there must be something extraordinary with this brand. Thus, such followers and the rituals they exercise can help the brand win new customers.

A creative director noted, "Cult brands never became cult brands because of great TV or print advertising campaigns, but because they were connected to a credible subculture that truly worshiped the brand. Nowadays, it is no secret that people mistrust traditional advertising messages. Therefore, advertising these days has to deliver true stories, real values, and show what brands make and how they add to the world." All of this is best communicated by cult brands' followings, as they are much more credible than conventional advertising messages.

Persistence

Besides subcultural origin, the theme of mass market also came up. A branding expert posited, "A cult brand arises in a very specific subculture, somewhere far away from the mainstream." However, a cult brand can also be a mass-market product, such as Nivea, Apple, and Havaianas for instance. Still, a chief executive officer claimed that "most cult brands today pretend to have a cult status; it is more pretending than it is anything else." Another participant disagreed: "A brand's cult status will always go with the brand. The cultic thing might be much stronger at the very beginning, as cult brands at that moment chiefly address specific members of subcultures or people that are affiliated with it. And as time passes and the cult brand becomes popular to more than just a specific subculture, it might lose some of its strong cult status, but it will always be a cult brand." A creative director noted, "A brand must not coercively lose its cult status just because it moves into the mass market. The same brand can still stand for the original values and lifestyle, and thus still be a cult brand." Another creative director agreed, stating that "a cult brand can totally be in the mainstream, like Apple or Red Bull. However, they should make sure not to lose their connection to their original cultural meaning and to what they stand for. For the followers of Red Bull, to see Red Bull offering cellular products and services is not brand consistent, and out of context. I mean that would be the same as Apple suddenly entering the food industry and supplying pizza and spaghetti."

Another chief creative officer weighed in on this point, arguing that "it's hard for a cult brand to maintain that sort of cult status as it gets bigger." He took the view that many brands wear out their cult status, but he also pointed out that it is hard to say whether they have lost the cult status or not. A creative director came up with another very interesting point, arguing that "the cult status of a brand can only get lost if there is a new social shift happening, to which it failed to act or react properly."

It seems, then, that a cult brand can lose its cult status only when it is pushed away by a new cult brand. A brand consultant cited this dramatic example: "Nokia, once a cellphone pioneer, and undoubtedly a cult brand, was literally overrun by Apple." Nokia apparently slept through the cultural change, and that's why it is now struggling so hard to get back to where it once was. He went on to say, "Listen, it's the changes in the world, in society, in law, in politics, in every other field that can cause customers to lose interest in a brand." A creative culturalist and a chief executive officer both suggested that "there are so many changes in society and culture going on, a brand needs somebody saying, 'We are on a great run right now, but I think we have to be aware of these changes coming up.' We have to make that conscious effort to proactively or reactively shift our brand, but the latter is not going to be as good, and will be much more painful." One of the most pertinent examples in this context is Apple. It is one of the most brilliant brands when it comes to connecting branding with culture, particularly cultural change. A creative cultural director explained that "Apple knew that the society's culture was going to shift, and the cell phone became a much more important device than it used to be. They decided to enter this new market but decided that 'if we are going to make a cell phone it's got to be as great as the other products in the past.'" So Apple maintained their core values but was able to pivot, because they saw the cultural change coming. What would Apple be right now if they had not entered the music market with the iPod in 2001 and the cell phone market with the iPhone six years later? Most likely a niche brand.

3.3 Summary of Studies 1 and 2 and Definition of *Cult Brand*

To this point, two qualitative studies have been conducted. The key objective of these two studies was to get a better understanding of what constitutes a cult brand in the perception of consumers and experts. Study 1 and 2 can be summarized according to the five key characteristics that emerged. A cult brand's origin is to be found in a specific culture with a specific dominant ideology. Most often cult brands emerge as a small subculture promoting a viewpoint that is contrarian to the dominant ideology. To communicate this deviant ideology, a unique brand story has to be composed. This brand story acts as the common ground for conveying the ideology and gaining followers. Cult followers are a pivotal characteristic of a cult brand, since it's them spreading the word and "preaching for the brand." Lastly, a cult brand is persistent and can only lose its cult status when it loses its link to the connected subculture or misses significant cultural changes.

These five characteristics serve as a basis in providing an answer to what cult brands actually are. Thus, I define a cult brand as

> *a brand whose exceptionally strong and unique identity results from picking up on an emerging, yet popular sociocultural change. This helps form its novel ideology, thereby providing a specific group of people (i.e., a subculture) the opportunity to express themselves. This vanguard brand ideology conveyed through a unique story is the reason for the brand's ability to building up a large cult following.*

However, managers have asked how to create cult brands, which leads me to introduce the next chapter, where I answer this question by introducing the cult brand model.

4   The Cult Brand Model

The definition of a cult brand in conjunction with the five characteristics I introduced above lays down the basis for the development of the *cult brand model*. Putting these characteristics into chronological order enables me to derive model stages. The left column of Table 2 represents the five characteristics of a cult brand resulting from Study 1 and 2. The middle column lists key ideas from those two studies that link these characteristics to the model stage listed in the right column.

Characteristics	Ideas from Study 1 and Study 2 Illustrating the Link between Characteristics and the Model Stage	Model Stages
Cultural Origin	Origination after shift in society; based on counterculture; arise from culture; calling into question existing viewpoints; change the predominant culture; arise in a subculture and cause a cultural change; attack the predominant culture; against mainstream beliefs; explicit values and beliefs.	Detection of the Cultural Change
Vanguard Brand Ideology	Revolutionary idea; first to market; vanguard aspect of the product; innovative thinking; vanguard approach affect product category; a new way of thinking; totally new lifestyle.	Formulation of the Vanguard Brand Ideology

Characteristics	Ideas from Study 1 and Study 2 Illustrating the Link between Characteristics and the Model Stage	Model Stages
Unique Brand Story	Has been cultivated; the story matters; story must connect subcultural values with the brand; cultural story, not just a great story; communication of the ideology.	Creation of the Unique Brand Story
Cult Following	A certain group must convince others; must be attractive to more than just a few early followers; exclusivity because of specific values and lifestyles; cultic action; gaining more followers; word of mouth instead of advertising; starts in a small community and spreads from there.	Formation of the Cult Following
Persistence	Cultic aspect stronger at beginning; cult status can decrease; only fully lose cult status when new cultural change happening; need someone to prevent a brand from missing cultural changes.	Establishment of the Cultural-Change Orientation

Table 2: Coding Categories for the Cult Brand Model

The connecting strand joining all the aspects of the focus-group discussion with the expert interviews, is the strong emphasis on a cult brand's success at addressing sociocultural issues, which lead to changes in culture and society as shown in the above definition. Given the pivotal importance of cultural change to cult brands, it is all about staying alert to all possible shifts in society that could cause cultural changes. First, though, marketers must acquire a broad understanding of the dominant culture (i.e., ideology) in the relevant product category. Stage 1 in Figure 2 is precisely this first preparatory task of gaining a vivid awareness of a particular dominant ideology, its values and beliefs— *analysis of the predominant ideology.* Based on the results gained in that preparatory stage, marketers then must detect the emerging cultural change within this predominant culture—*detection of the cultural change* (see stage 2 in Figure 2).

While cult brands draw upon a specific cultural change and build the brand's ideology based on that change, both Study 1 and Study 2 showed that there are four other highly descriptive features of cult brands in addition to the aforementioned major characteristic—cultural change. One of these is *vanguard brand ideology*, which means being first to market with a specific cultural innovation. This does not only have to be the product; but it can be the mode of communication, design, layout, packaging, etc. So once the significant upcoming shift in culture and society has been detected, the next step is called *formulation of the vanguard brand ideology.* This ideology, along with the predominant ideology, consists of values, beliefs, and a specific lifestyle that lays down the basis for the vanguard brand ideology (see stage 3 in Figure 2).

Another characteristic that also emerges from both studies is *unique brand story*. This is all about the rich story that connects the brand with the culture or subculture and thus endows it with cultural meaning. A brand story in this context must meet high requirements in order to convey values. This is done in the third stage: *creation of the unique brand story* (see stage 4 in Figure 2).

Both consumers and experts saw cult brands as having devoted followings. It reminds us that a cult brand has some extremely emotionally attached customers who could even be considered as the brand's devoted following. At this particular stage, true believers and devoted followers have to be found and imbued with the brand's ideology—*formation of the cult following* (see stage 5 in Figure 2).

The last characteristic I observed in my qualitative research relates to a cult brand's persistence. My results reveal that although a cult status can decrease, it cannot get completely lost. Indeed, the fifth stage deals with precisely such prevention. The cultural-change orientation of a cult brand must be established in the brand management—*establishment of the cultural-change orientation* (see stage 6 in Figure 2). These six stages constitute the cult brand model presented in Figure 2. The following five subchapters are dedicated to the six stages of the cult brand model.

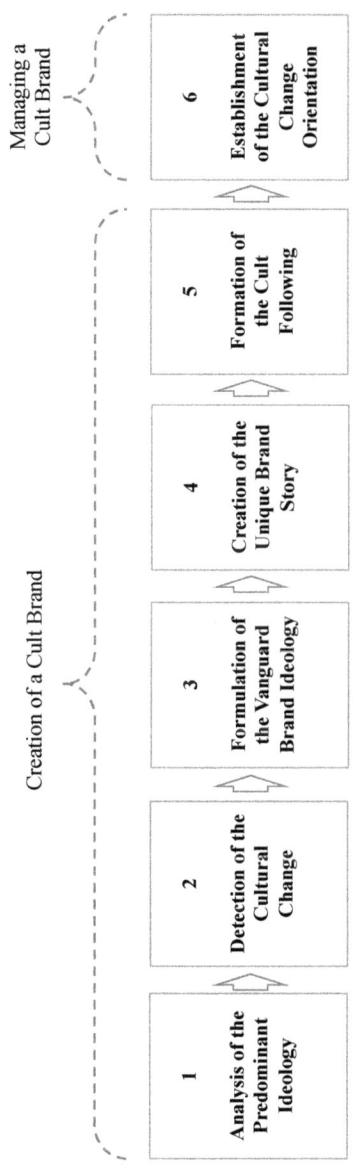

Figure 2: The Cult Brand Model

4.1 Preparatory Stage 1: Analysis of the Predominant Ideology

The consumer interviews as well as the interviews with experts showed that a cult brand mostly emerges from a countercultural movement imbued with a specific ideology. In other words, the movement arises out of cultural change. In order to detect such a change, a brand must first get to know the predominant cultural values and beliefs. Thus, this first stage is about attaining a comprehensive understanding of the cultural standard (i.e., predominant ideology) of the particular product category. According to Geertz (1973), culture is a symbolic system based upon ideological principles, which encompass the consumers' beliefs and values. There are many different ideologies that exist within groups or classes of people, though usually there is one specific ideology that is superior—conceived as normative, the most popular and accepted way of thinking (Eagleton 1991; Hirschman 1988). This is a society's predominant ideology, its cultural standard. By decoding this predominant ideology, as it exists within every marketplace or product category, brand managers can understand the values and beliefs held by their customers (Eagleton 1991). Knowing these values and beliefs rather than the customers' explicit needs, which arise from values and beliefs, marketers gain the ability to detect possible shifts in society and culture—changes in culture that contradict the prevailing one and thus do not just create products but combine them with the new relevant cultural meaning. As a consequence, brand managers who have steeped themselves in the predominant culture of a product category, marketplace, or sector can proceed to construct a branding strategy that takes full account of such cultural meanings. Even more excitingly, they can create strategies that consciously contradict this predominant ideology and thereby bring something new into the marketplace. In order to demonstrate what such a predominant culture is, let us go back for a moment to the "good life" as it was lived in America after World War II. At that time, people had a great desire to have the newest, most technologically advanced products. This value system was reflected perfectly by the American automobile industry, which offered vehicles suitable to each ascending step of the status ladder. Detroit promoted cars in a glamorous context, its advertising emphasizing the great new features, gadgets, technological components, comforts, and power. Thus the automobile industry's predominant ideology clearly purveyed an ethos of showing off one's status, living beyond one's means (see Figure 3).

Figure 3: General Motors Advertisement for its Five Car Brands from the 1960s[3]

---

[3] Source: www.oldcaradvertising.com

By questioning the prevailing ethos in the car industry, and turning the market upside down, it is plausible that Volkswagen analyzed and understood this predominant ideology in the car industry and consciously attacked it by launching the Beetle (see Baritz 1988; Holt 2004; Kiley 2002).

Figure 4: Volkswagen Beetle Advertisement from the 1960s[4]

---

[4] Text in the advertisement: "Think small. Our little car isn't so much of a novelty any more. A couple of dozen college kids don't try to squeeze inside it. The guy at the gas station doesn't ask where the gas goes. Nobody even stares at our shape. In fact, some people who drive our little

4.2   Stage 2: The Detection of the Cultural Change

This next stage, which comes after having analyzed the predominant ideology and being aware of its values and beliefs, is dedicated to figuring out which values and beliefs are subject to such a shift. One factor accounting for cultural and social changes is economic development. It occurs in most societies and causes such direct changes as occupational specialization, rising educational levels, and rising income levels and thus leads to increased wealth (Inglehart and Baker 2000). But aside from these predictable changes, economic development might also lead to less predictable changes—that is to say, changes in culture—such as in gender roles (e.g., emancipation), in attitudes toward sexual norms (e.g., gay-rights movement), and in personality traits (e.g., narcissism). In sum, unlike economic principles, cultural change does not take a predictable linear path. Hence the need for marketers to analyze emerging subcultures and figure out which path the changes might take becomes a crucial undertaking.

Those responsible for the changes in cultural meaning, which arise out of oppositional ideologies, are people who live out on the fringe of society, jointly comprising a group that differentiates itself from the mainstream culture. It is such subcultures or cults that trigger the development of novel ideologies (Bainbridge and Stark 1979; Blumberg 1974; Field 1970; Meyerson and Katz 1957). Such subcultures pursue a deviant ideology, which they think superior to the surrounding one, and they are willing to engage for a change.

---

flivver don't even think 32 miles to the gallon is going any great guns. Or using five pints of oil instead of five quarts. Or never needing anti-freeze. Or racking up 40,000 miles on a set of tires. That's because once you get used to some of our economies, you don't even think about them anymore. Except when you squeeze into a small parking spot. Or renew your small insurance. Or pay a small repair bill. Or trade in your old VW for a new one. Think it over."
Source: www.adforum.com

Even a few decades ago, Georg Lois (2012, p. 16), an advertising legend for the last couple decades, was aware of the importance of cultural change:

Great graphic and verbal communication depends on under-standing and adapting to the culture, anticipating the culture, criticizing changes in the culture, and helping to change the culture. Any entrepreneur, inventor, artist, graphic designer, adman, fashion designer, architect, editor, doctor, lawyer, politician—anyone who instinctively feels the way to go is against a conservative, indoctrinated society and bucks the trend, and who understands the zeitgeist of the time—has the passion and capability to become a cultural provocateur. So if you're a young person with an entrepreneurial spirit who aspires to succeed, not only in business, but in life, your mission is not to sedate, but to awaken, to disturb, to communi-cate, to command, to instigate, and even to provoke.

The following example of Whole Foods illustrates this phenomenon of cultural change in a comprehensible way: In the postindustrial era of the mid-1990s, people began to reject the economic growth at "any price" mentality and in-stead began to place greater value on quality of life, self-expression, and envi-ronmental protection (Bell 1973; Inglehart 1997; Inglehart and Baker 2000; Lesthaeghe 1983). More specifically, when consumers became aware of the commercial food industry's questionable practices with respect to both animal husbandry and the use of pesticides and chemicals to grow vegetables and fruits, a countercultural movement arose in opposition to the modes of conven-tional food production. This countermovement embraced those new values, and owing to their acceptance and their power, this initiated a cultural change and hence disturbed or even replaced the predominant ideology. As a consequence of this change more and more people, driven by a concern for both personal health and animal welfare, demand all-natural or even organic foods. This change has led to sales growth of up to 20 percent a year for organic food through the early 2000s (Hansen 2004). Whole Foods picked up on this evolution and delivered the sought-after cultural meaning of healthiness, which accounts for its exponential growth over the last decade and its impressive entrance into the mass market.

Apart from Whole Foods, Nike also acts as a perfect case illustrating the stage 2, cultural change. In the late 1970s, America got hit by a large recession (Bluestone and Harrison 1984; Harrison and Bluestone 1990). Everyone had to fight in order to survive in this challenging new economic situation, and that demanded an entirely different mentality: individualism was back. People wanted to condition their bodies and minds so that they could compete in the new, more competitive labor market. Jogging as an individual sport gained many devotees because it made sense to tens of millions of Americans. While other brands still used star athletes in their advertising, Nike drew upon this cultural change to convey the runner's ideology, the very thing that would later become the brand's ideological foundation: *solo willpower*. Its advertising firm, Wieden+Kennedy, purveyed this ideology in 1988 by launching the first "Just Do It." This new ideology, translated as "No matter who you are, no matter what your physical, economic, or social limitations, transcendence is not just possible, it is waiting to be called forth. Take control of your life and don't submit to the mundane forces that can so easily weigh us down in daily life. No more rationalizations and justifications, it's time to act" (Goldman and Papsons 1990, p. 19). Nike wanted people to confront and to overcome any barrier. Nike even went beyond the world of sports. Wieden+Kennedy's advertisement alluded to various types of societal discrimination, such as racism, sexism, and global poverty. These gave guidance to people facing the new rough new global economy—Nike's future customers (Goldman and Papson 1990; Holt 2004; Holt and Cameron 2010).

4.3   Stage 3: The Formulation of the Vanguard Brand Ideology

Each group or class of people (i.e., society) has its own ideology, a set of values and beliefs (Eagleton 1991; Hirschman 1988; 1993; Thompson 1984). The ideology is the meaning system of a brand (Atkin 2004) or as Holt and Cameron (2010, p. 174) describe it, "the particular point of view on a cultural construct that is central to the product." The goal is then to define the novel ideology based on the illuminated cultural change and formulate the cult brand's system of thoughts, values, and beliefs. I noted earlier that a vital task within this process, the building of a cult brand, is that of carefully analyzing a particular subculture's identity-project—the values, beliefs, and ways of life of those who live within that subculture (McCracken 1986). The expression of cultural meaning plays a fundamental role particularly in bringing together abstract values and specific consumer attitudes, their goals, and how they behave (Aaker 2000; Kamakura and Novak 1992; Peng, Nisbett, and Wong 1997; Richins 1994).

A brand conveying a novel ideology becomes a cult brand because it takes the risk of thinking outside the box and thus becomes vanguard. It is crucial to be first to market—which is to say, to be a pioneer. A cult brand and its products inspire consumers not just by delivering a high level of creativity and innovation (Holt and Cameron 2010; Ragas and Bueno 2002) but also by being first to market with the claim, the design, the message, the functionality, or the communication. It is by blending those two attributes that the brand obtains a certain cultic position in the market.

Anita Roddick was a true pioneer when it comes to supplying people with sustainable products. In 1976, inspired by the original The Body Shop in California, she opened her own shop in the United Kingdom. Roddick had anticipated the cultural change at a time long before green issues became fashionable. By taking advantage of the societal shift toward sustainability, The Body Shop started to inspire millions of consumers to change the way they think. The Unilever brand Dove has also picked up on this social problem and has called into question the modeling industry, Photoshopping beautiful women, and promoting products via superskinny models (Smeesters, Mussweiler, and Mandel 2010). From its very beginning, The Body Shop expressed a specific cultural meaning and this is what enabled it to bring sustainable products to the mass market. In the early 1990s, it entered into an alliance with Greenpeace to save whales and promote renewable energy. The brand also expanded its cultural expression to embrace social issues such as bulimia and anorexia. Its management launched campaigns designed to counteract the stereotyping of women as skinny models and to raise their self-esteem. The Body Shop positioned itself as a social and environmental pioneer. To date, the main success factor of The Body Shop has undoubtedly been its vanguard, pioneering ideology that supports community fair trade, defends human rights, fights against animal testing, activates self-esteem, and protects our planet (Our History 2013) at a time when a general shift in society toward those values had started (Aaker 1996; Atkin 2004).

As with The Body Shop, Starbucks is also a great example when it comes to illustrating the vanguard brand ideology. Starbucks revolutionized the coffee market through transforming gourmet coffee from a yuppie status to a mainstream product (Thompson and Arsel 2004). Before Starbucks, coffee was just coffee to Americans. They knew nothing about beans—their origin or how they are grown. Then, too, the taste of coffee was the same across myriad retailers such as McDonald's, Dunkin' Donuts, and such grocery-store chains as 7-Eleven and White Hen Pantry. From 1965 to 1975, however, there was a large increase in the number of Americans graduating from college. Thus that generation was much more sophisticated as compared to earlier ones. It was those young people who first began to demand more developed food culture, which meant that grocery stores had to start stocking arugula, heirloom tomatoes, edamame, and free-range chicken (McCracken 2012; Sherry 1995). Since the 1990s, there has been enormous growth in businesses that offer consumers a chance to express their sophistication (e.g., Whole Foods Market and Design Within Reach; Holt and Cameron 2010). This subculture based on respect for seasonal and locally grown agricultural products has questioned and challenged the industrial food culture. The industrial ideology meant mass scale, machine made, and cheap, whereas the new artisanal, cosmopolitan vanguard ideology conveys values such as handcrafted, small lots, and "whatever the best costs." The coffee shops that have sprung up everywhere have literally become homes for artists, writers, musicians, and other members of the cultural elite. It was to service this subculture that the new "boutique" retail stores were designed. Its ideology of serving high-quality coffee was picked up by many competitors and thus made Starbucks a pioneer (Holt and Cameron 2010; Schultz and Gordon 2012; Thompson and Arsel 2004).

4.4   Stage 4: The Creation of the Unique Brand Story

It is beyond contention that brands seeking to be successful must be good at product quality, design, distribution, pricing, customer service, etc. However, these aspects are simply the prerequisites of being competitive. They are not drivers to achieve cult status (Holt 2004). Cult brands only thrive through wise communication strategies and using advertising as a powerful instrument to transfer meaning from the culturally constituted world to a product and from the product to the individual consumer (McCracken 1986). First and foremost it is through advertisements imbued with cultural meaning that marketers con-vey new ideologies (Belk and Pollay 1985; Hirschman 1988; McCracken 1986; Thompson and Haytko 1997). Advertisements provide consumers with valued information on desirable manners, styles, entertainments, and lifestyles (Holder 1973). The success of a cult brand's communication depends, howev-er, not only on the message it presents but also on how well the message con-veys the brand's desirable ideology (McCracken 1989; Hirschman and Thompson 1997). In other words, a rich story is key. Often this story related to the creation of the brand, its traditions, its rivalry against competitors, its cus-tomers, or simply its products (Beverland 2009). Such a story to be credible must be firmly founded upon the problems of a particular subculture and the clever solution to them that the brand represents (Slotkin 1973). All of which means that the brand managers of a cult brand must identify their most appro-priate story and link it to pertinent cultural change (Holt 2004). The brand's success depends ultimately on the creation of a distinctive cultural tradition and the proper use of metaphors (Slotkin 1973). Moreover, the story should be a strong communicator of the defined ideology (Atkin 2004). Since communi-ties also are crucial to the success of cult brands, they most likely are formed around brands that have a "strong image, a rich and lengthy history, and threatening competition" (Muñiz and O'Guinn 2001, p. 415).

Holt (2004) asserts that in order to create an iconic brand, one must "apply the art of storytelling to the commercial format of advertising." This is also true for cult brands. Stories are a perfect way to bring the defined ideology to life—perfect carriers of ideologies. By means of a well-crafted story, an advertising message can gain in richness of cultural meaning and thus become a compelling transmitter of meaning. For a cult brand, however, storytelling means more than just communicating a funny, exciting, and compelling story. A cult brand's story needs to convey the specific subcultural ideology. It is furthermore crucial to draw on a subculture's source material when a brand manager is developing a story. But because in the case of most of the established brands there is a lot of substantial "source material" available and it only has to be uncovered (Holt 2004), the storytelling remains the most important instrument to transfer cultural meaning. Hence this is the fact why it has been so widely examined in academic literature (Barker and Gower 2010; Brown, Kozinets, and Sherry 2003; Grover 2009; Gunelius 2013; Herskovitz and Crystal 2010; Patterson and Brown 2005; Simmons 2006; Woodside 2010; Woodside, Sood, and Miller 2008).

Among beer brands, Corona is the only one whose story has served to connect it to its subculture of origin. When the "good life" of the postwar era had become a thing of the past and work had become much more competitive, as outsourcing and process engineering were implemented, getting away from "all that hassle at work" became a strong cultural desire of lower- and middle-class folks (Gordon 1996; Phillips 1993). Corona wisely launched a story, all about escaping from everyday routines, that was tremendously appealing to hardworking Americans. The ad campaigns of the mid-1990s showed an idyllic Mexican beach where a couple, lying in long chairs, is staring out at the sea and listening to the waves while two Coronas stand on a table between them. Thus Corona became one of the most powerful expressions of relaxation to Americans, due to a cultural change, a change in the workload of the average American worker (Baritz 1988; Holt 2004).

4.5   Stage 5: The Formation of the Cult Following

In many cases, cult brands have customers that literally act like evangelists or preachers, spreading positive messages about the brand and actively trying to convince and recruit other customers (Ahuvia 2005; Brady et al. 2004; Hyken 2009; Pimentel and Reynolds 2004). Such highly devoted followers worship the brand to an extreme extent in the sense that they are passionate about the brand and all associations that come with it. Such followers in fact feel the need to share their emotions and to help others to "finally see the wonder of it" (Matzler, Pichler, and Hemetsberger 2007; Rozanski, Baum, and Wolfsen 1999). Thus a cult brand must successfully acquire a devoted following— virtually a cult-like following—who have an extraordinary emotional attach-ment to the brand (Chalfant, Beckley, and Palmer 1986; Langone 1993). The strong relationship between these customers and the brand becomes an im-portant part of their lives. As compared with a *cult brand*, a *brand cult* "is meant to describe a strong connection with a group of cognitively initiated individuals" (Acosta and Devasagayam 2010, p. 166). The brand manager's crucial task, therefore, is to set up a strategy based on that specific subgroup, which nonetheless manages to influence prospective consumers and promote the brand via convincing arguments (Wells 2001).

Surely the best example in this regard is Harley-Davidson and especially the Harley Owners Group (HOG). After World War II, many veterans
joined motorcycle clubs to create an alternative social world—a countercultural scene based on biking. These primarily lower-class men were inspired by
American outlaws and lived the outlaw ideology; they knew how to fend for
themselves and to fight for whatever they needed. This lifestyle, so contrary to
the timidly conformist values of modern society, persisted through many cultural and societal changes from 1950 onward. Even now the motorcycle clubs
remain the same, still sticking to their outlaw ideals. In the late 1970s, however, another remarkable cultural shift happened. Although mainly embodied in
the hippie culture, middle-class Americans also began to favor a progressive
ideology consisting of ecology, feminism, and civil rights. At the same time,
lower-class white people were struggling, because America's manufacturing
industry had entered into a new era of deindustrialization. Thus, these men had
to find something to hold on to. The "real manhood" ideology of the outlaw
bikers was now confronted by a new enemy: the privileged middle-class hippies (Aaker 1996; Holt 2004). We must remember that the economic crisis of
the early 1980s also hit middle-class men, many of whom lost their jobs and
along with them their authority, prestige, and identity. When Bill Clinton was
elected president in 1992, he pursued new-economy values, which was contrary to what the middle class desired. By then, however, President Reagan's
conservative vision—essentially a gunfighter ideology—had seized the public's, and especially the male public's, imagination. This time, however, to a
much larger extent, now extending across a broad pattern of America's mass
culture. The time was ripe for Harley-Davidson to become a convincing symbol of the Reagan ideology. The bike gained, seemingly overnight, an enormous popularity among politically conservative, middle-class white men. Thus

the brand gained cult status because it was able to solve the societal tensions felt by men who found themselves confronted by the American economic restructuring of the 1990s (Hill and Rifkin 1999; Holt 2004; Wayland and Cole 1997).

Harley-Davidson is, therefore, the perfect example of how a devoted following can strengthen the brand's values and communicate them in an authentic, credible, and convincing way.

4.6 Stage 6: The Establishment of the Cultural-Change Orientation

While stages 1 to 5 are dedicated to the creation of cult brands, this last stage deals with managing the cult brand. As we learned earlier, the cult brand model is highly dependent on an accurate evaluation of a current product-category-specific culture. In other words, the new ideology can be created properly thanks to the first two stages only, where the predominant culture is analyzed and the cultural change is identified. But what happens once the cult brand has been established? As both studies revealed, cult brands are persistent. Nevertheless, cult status can diminish once a cult brand has entered the mass market. However, the only way a brand can fully lose its cult status is, by ignoring new shifts in society and cultural changes (e.g., Nokia, Kodak, Saab Automobile). We are reminded here yet again of the crucial importance of being aware of losing cult status, if they are to be properly managed and thereby prevented from losing their cult status. Thus it is pivotal if a brand wants to maintain its cult status for managers to keep track of significant changes in society and culture.

McCracken (2012) introduced the idea of the chief culture officer. He takes the view that without the knowledge of cultural changes going on in a society, a brand is likely to miss opportunities or even fail entirely. He points to how Microsoft failed to see the cultural change away from conventional personal computers to more creative machines—such as tablets, search engines, and social media—and has struggled ever since to catch up. Google (free Web-based software), Apple (importance of mobile devices), and Facebook (social interaction and communication) have overtaken Microsoft because they accurately assessed the cultural evolution and thereby addressed the needs of their current and prospective customers. Apart from Microsoft, there are other examples why successful businesses at some point failed over the last decades. A missed cultural shift can be one of the reasons why big companies failed. Culture should receive the same importance as other functions in a company, such as management, finance, strategic planning, and human resources (McCracken 2012).

5 Conclusion and Discussion

There are many approaches to branding. Some of them are based on functional or emotional benefits. Others are focused on social experience or personal traits. There is no branding model that takes full-enough account of cultural change. There's evidence enough that culture is not only a vital influencer for new brands but also for existing brands. Indeed, also the scholar Nassim Nicholas Taleb in his new book *The Antifragile* (2013) reasserts that the world is changing much faster than it used to. Taleb asks us to accept this turmoil as the new order of things. Culture is a crucial part of these changes and in many cases is the cause. Such cultural changes are the triggers for new cult brands, as we have seen with the cases of Nike, Starbucks, and Harley-Davidson, which are some of the most powerful brands in the Western world. Their success is not based solely on product features or innovations. Nike is not successful because they have engineered the best shoes. Its competitors also did a great job, but none of them has succeeded to the same extent as Nike. Similarly, Starbucks is not the world's best-known coffee brand due to its exceptional coffee; Harley-Davidson is not successful because of its famous engine roar. It is no easy matter, however, to gain a clear-cut understanding of these cult brands. In most cases, the academic as well as the managerial literature lacks consistent and well-founded definitions of cult brands. However, based on this analysis, these brands seem to have succeeded on a grand scale not because they offered great products or implemented innovative strategies but simply because they built their brands on a cultural (change) context, as marketers were able to offer their customers a value-based proposition inclusive of its culture-based meaning relative to personal needs. These factors serve as the underlying foundation of the cult brand model I have proposed.

In this study, I investigated the phenomenon of cult brands, showing what constitutes a cult brand and how cult brands can be developed. Based on a widespread literature review on cultures, cults, and subcultures, as well as two major qualitative studies, I have shown that sensitivity to *cultural change* is the most widely shared characteristic of cult brands and thus must be the focus of any viable cult brand strategy. We also have seen how cultural changes are always triggered by specific subcultures or by cults from a more religious perspective. Beyond these major characteristics, I have also noted that four additional characteristics play an important role in creating and sustaining cult brands: vanguard ideology, unique brand story, cult following, and persistence. Putting these characteristics into a dynamic perspective has delivered the six-stage cult brand model.

In the first, preparatory stage, the task is to analyze the predominant ideology. This provides the marketer with the necessary knowledge of the product category's specific culture. The second stage is about identifying the cultural change. Marketers should intuit an imminent change in society affecting culture and hence the brand. In the third stage, the vanguard brand ideology is created. Now one has to define, in detail, the cultural ideology and its values and beliefs based on the cultural change. The fourth stage is all about communicating the unique brand story. In the fifth stage, devoted brand followers are gained. Finally, the last stage is dedicated to ensuring that future changes in the culture are detected and that brand managers are ready in advance to cope with them instead of being forced to react.

Cult brands are an opportunity to grow market share, gain higher profits, and achieve a price premium (Carr 1996; Dawling 2004). It is apparent that building cult brands is a strategy that pays off. The results of this research not only raised consciousness about the characteristics of a cult brand but also made the phenomenon more "tangible." Most importantly, however, the results offer a stage model of how to build up such a powerful cult brand. While the first five stages of the cult brand model help managers to navigate through the process of creating a cult brand, the last stage anchors the cultural-change orientation as a core function in brand management. McCracken (2012) even takes this last function further and suggests building the function of a cultural chief officer—CCO. Both parts of the cult brand model illustrate the very basis for considering cultural factors in strategic branding decisions when creating new brands as well as when managing existing brands. Its results show that executives need to be aware of the impact of culture for their branding endeavors, irrespective of building cult brands or normal brands. The model and its conceptualization stress that managers' failures to understand such cultural changes can jeopardize brand images and identities of existing brands. In other words, a lack of interest in cultural changes by successful brand managers can lead to being undercut by emerging cult brands. For this reason, it becomes highly important for brand management to develop and employ tools that help them understand culture and society. Such an understanding helps brands to promote an ideology linked to cultural and subcultural contexts. As a consequence, branding concepts such as brand equity and brand value should be extended by cultural and sociocultural components.

In this research, mainly well-known "global" cult brands such as Apple, Harley-Davidson, and IKEA have been considered. I have not considered less-known local cult brands. I assume that there is a dynamic perspective, meaning that a cult brand starts as totally unknown, slowly growing awareness in its subculture and eventually succeeding in making the step into the mainstream. Against this background, it remains unclear at what point of time a brand is a cult brand. So further research could focus on the dynamic perspective of cult

70

brands, investigating at which moment in time brands have become cult brands and when, if at all, they have become iconic brands.

Another interesting point for future research on cult brands could address the product category. Based on social consumption and self-expression factors, I would assume that the cult brand model works best for brands with a high self-expression potential. However, with regard to ideology and value theories, which suggest a more intrinsic perspective, less-self-expressive brands such as body care products, toothpaste, and detergent could also become cult brands.

References

Aaker, David A. (1996), *Building Strong Brands*, The Free Press: New York.

Aaker, David A. (2009), Beyond Functional Benefits, *Marketing News*, September (30), 23.

Aaker, Jennifer L. (1997), Dimensions of Brand Personality, *Journal of Marketing Research*, 34 (3), 347–56.

Aaker, Jennifer L. (1999), The Malleable Self: The Role of Self-Expression in Persuasion, *Journal of Marketing Research*, 36 (1), 45–57.

Aaker, Jennifer L. (2000), Accessibility or Diagnosticity? Disentangling the Influence of Culture on Persuasion Processes, *Journal of Consumer Research*, 26 (March), 340–357.

Acosta, Paul M. and Raj Devasagayam (2010), Brand Cult: Extending the Notion of Brand Communities, *Marketing Management Journal*, 20 (Spring), 165–176.

Ahuvia, Aaron C. (2005), Beyond the Extended Self: Loved Objects and Consumers' Identity Narratives, *Journal of Consumer Research*, 32 (June), 171–184.

Amaldoss, Wilfred and Sanjay Jain (2005), Conspicuous Consumption and Sophisticated Thinking, *Management Science*, 51 (10), 1449–1466.

Appel, Willa (1983), *Cults in America*, New York: Holt, Reinhart, and Winston.

Arnold, Matthew (1996), Culture and Anarchy, in *What is Cultural Studies? A Reader,* John Storey, ed., London: Arnold, 6–11.

Arnould, Eric J. and Craig J. Thompson (2005), Consumer Culture Theory (CCT): Twenty Years of Research, *Journal of Consumer Research,* 31 (4), 868–882.

Atkin, Douglas (2004), The Culting of Brands: When Customer Become True Believers, New York: Portfolio.

Bainbridge, William S. and Rodney Stark (1979), Cult Formation: Three Compatible Models, *Sociological Analysis*, 40 (4), 283–295.

Barber, Bernard and Lyle Lobel (1953), Fashion in Women's Clothing and the American Social System, in *Class and Status and Power,* Reinhard Bendix and Seymour M. Lipset, eds., New York: The Free Press, 323–332.

Baritz, Lauren (1988), The Good Life—The Meaning of Success for the American Middle Class, New York: Knopf.

Barker, Randolph und Kim Gower (2010), Strategic Application of Storytelling in Organizations—Toward Effective Communication in a Diverse World, *Journal of Business Communication,* 47 (3), 295–312.

Baudrillard, Jean (1998), *The Consumer Society: Myths and Structures,* Newbury, CA: Sage Publications.

Belk, Russel W. (1988), Possessions and the Extended Self, *Journal of Consumer Research,* 15 (September), 139-168.

Belk, Russel W. (1989), Effects of Identification with Comic Book Heroes and Villains of Consumption on Materialism among Former Comic Book Readers, *Advances in Consumer Research*, 16, 414–419.

Belk, Russel W. and Richard W. Pollay (1985), Images of Ourselves: The Good Life in Twentieth Century Advertising, *Journal of Consumer Research,* 11 (March), 887–897.

Belk, Russell W., Melanie Wallendorf, and John F. Sherry, Jr. (1989), The Sacred and the Profane in Consumer Behavior: Theodicy on the Odyssey, *Journal of Consumer Research,* 16 (June), 1–38.

Belk, Russel W. and Gülnur Tumbat (2005), The Cult of Macintosh, *Consumption, Markets and Culture*, 8 (3), 205–217.

Bell, Daniel (1973), *The Coming of Post-Industrial Society*, New York: Basic Books.

Berthon, Pierre, Morris B. Holbrook, James M. Hulbert, and Leyland F. Pitt (2007), Viewing Brands in Multiple Dimensions, *MIT Sloan Management Review,* 48 (2), 36–44.

Berger, Jonah and Chip Heath (2007), Where Consumers Diverge from Others: Identity Signaling and Product Domains, *Journal of Consumer Research*, 34 (2), 121–134.

Beverland, Michael (2009), Building Brand Authenticity: 7 Habits of Iconic Brands, New York: Palgrave Macmillan.

Blackston, Max (1992), Observations: Building Brand Equity by Managing the Brand's Relationships, *Journal of Advertising Research,* 32 (3), 79–83.

Bluestone, Barry and Bennett Harrison (1984), *The Deindustrialization of America,* New York: Basic Books.

Blumberg, Paul (1974), The Decline and Fall of the Status Symbol: Some Thoughts on Status in a Post-Industrial Society, *Social Problems*, 21 (April), 480–498.

Boatwright, Josh (2013, October 30), Trader Joe's Opening St. Pete Store in 2014, St. Petersburg Tribune, retrieved on November 3, 2013, from http://tbo.com/pinellas-county/trader-joes-opening-st-pete-store-in-2014-20131030/.

Brady, Diane, Robert D. Hof, Andy Reinhardt, Moon Ihlwan, Stanley Holmes, and Kerry Capell (2004), Cult Brands, *Business Week*, August (2894), 65–67.

Brooks, David (2013, May 31), The Romantic Advantage, *The New York Times*, p. A21.

Brown, Stephen, Robert V. Kozinets und John F. Sherry, Jr. (2003), Teaching Old Brands New Tricks: Retro Branding and the Revival of Brand Meaning, *Journal of Marketing*, 67 (3), 19–33.

Buttle, Francis (1991), What People Do with Advertising, *International Journal of Advertising,* 10 (2), 95–110.

Calder, Bobby J. (1977), Focus Groups and the Nature of Qualitative Marketing Research, *Journal of Marketing Research*, 14 (August), 353-364.

Chalfant, Paul H., Robert E. Beckley, and Eddie C. Palmer (1986), *Religion in Contemporary Society*, Palo Alto: Mayfield.

Chaudhuri, Arjun and Morris B. Holbrook (2001), The Chain of Effects from Brand Trust and Brand Affect Brand Performance: The Role of Brand Loyalty, *Journal of Marketing,* 65 (2), 81–93.

Cleveland, Mark and Michel Laroche (2007), Acculturation of the Global Consumer Culture: Scale Development and Research Paradigm, *Impact of Culture on Marketing Strategy,* (60) 3, 249–259.

Collins, John J. (1991), The Cult Experience: An Overview of Cults, Their Traditions, and Why People Join Them, Illinois: Springfield.

Cult (n.d.), in *Merriam Webster's online dictionary*, retrieved on August 24, 2013, from http://www.merriam-webster.com/dictionary/cult.

Cova Bernard and Véronique Cova (2002), Tribal Marketing—The Tribalisation of Society and its Impact on the Conduct of Marketing, *The European Journal of Marketing*, 36 (5/6), 595–620.

Dowling, Bob (2004, August 8), The Rise of The Cult Brand, *Bloomberg Business Week Magazine*, retrieved on October 25, 2013, from http://www.businessweek.com/printer/articles/186848-rise-of-the-cult-brand?type=old_article.

Dawson, Lorne I. (2006), Comprehending Cults, the Sociology of New Religious Movements, Oxford: University Press.

Deshpandé, Rohit (1983), Paradigms Lost: On Theory and Method in Research in Marketing, *Journal of Marketing*, 47 (4), 101–110.

de Chernatony, Leslie and Francesca Dall'Olmo Riley (1998), Defining A "Brand:" Beyond The Literature With Experts' Interpretations, *Journal of Marketing Management,* 14 (5), 417–443.

Diamond, Nina, John F. Sherry, Jr., Albert M. Muñiz, Jr., Mary Ann McGrath, Robert V. Kozinets, and Stefania Borghini (2009), American Girl and the Brand Gestalt: Closing the Loop on Sociocultural Branding Research, *Journal of Marketing*, 7 (May), 118–134.

Douglas, Mary and Baron Isherwood (1979), *The World of Goods,* New York: Basic Books.

du Gay, Paul, Stuart Hall., Linda Janes, Hugh Mackay, and Keith Negus (1997), *Doing Cultural Studies: The Story of the Sony Walkman*, London: Sage Publications.

Durkheim, Émile (1968), Les Formes Élémentaires de la Vie Religieuse: Le Système Totémique en Australie, Livre 3, Paris: Press Universitaire.

Eagleton, Terry (1991), *Ideology: An Introduction*, Finland: WS Bookwell.

Elliot, Richard (1997), Existential Consumption and Irrational Desire, *European Journal of Marketing,* 34 (4), 285–296.

Elliot, Richard and Kritsadarat Wattanasuwan (1998), Brands as Symbolic Resources for the Construction of Identity, *Journal of Advertising,* 17, 131–144.

Ellwood, Robert S., Jr. (1987), *Many Peoples, Many Faiths,* Englewood Cliffs: Prentice-Hall.

Enroth, Ronald (1979), *The Lure of the Cults,* Chappaqua: Christian Herald.

Escalas, Jennifer E. and James R. Bettman (2003), You Are What They Eat: The Influence of Reference Groups on Consumer Connections to Brands, *Journal of Consumer Psychology,* 13 (3), 339–348.

Fallers, Lloyd A. (1961), A Note on the Trickle Effect, in *Sociology: Progress of a Decade,* Seymour M. Lipset and N. Smelser, eds., Englewood Cliffs, New Jersey: Prentice-Hall, 501–506

Fern, Edward F. (1982), The Use of Focus Groups for Idea Generation: The Effects of Group Size, Acquaintanceship, and Moderator on Response Quantity and Quality, *Journal of Marketing Research,* 19 (1), 1–13.

Field, George A. (1970), The Status Float Phenomenon: The Upward Diffusion of Innovation, *Business Horizons,* 13 (August), 45–52.

Gabriel, Yiannis and Tim Lang (1995), The Unmanageable Consumer: Contemporary Consumption and its Fragmentation, London: Sage Publications.

Geertz, Clifford (1973), *The Interpretation of Cultures,* New York: Basic Books.

Glaser, Barney and Anselm Strauss (1967), *The Discovery of Grounded Theory,* Chicago: Aldine.

Gobe, Marc (2001), Emotional Branding: *The New Paradigm for Connecting Brands to People,* New York: Allworth Press.

Goldman Robert and Papson Stephan (1990), *Nike Culture: The Sign of the Swoosh,* Thousand Oaks, California: Sage Publications.

Goodyear, Mary (1993), Reviewing the Concept of Brands and Branding, *Marketing and Research Today*, 21 (2), 75–79.

Gordon, David M. (1996), Fat and Mean: The Corporate Squeeze of Working Americans and the Myth of Managerial "Downsizing," New York: Free Press.

Gross, Jaime (2009, June 14), Save or Splurge: San Francisco, *The New York Times,* p. TR7.

Grover, Roland (2009), Selling by Storytelling: Jeff Gomez's Clients Such as Disney, Coke and Mattel Use his Narratives to Expand their Franchises, *Business Week,* 4132, 48–49.

Gunelius, Susan (February, 2013), 5 Secrets to Use Storytelling for Brand Marketing Success, *Forbes Magazine,* retrieved on June 15, 2013, from http://www.forbes.com/sites/work-in-progress/2013/02/05/5-secrets-to-using-storytelling-for-brand-marketing-success/.

Hansen, Nanette (2004, December 3), Organic Food Sales See Healthy Growth, *NBC News*, retrieved on June 6, 2013 from http://www.nbcnews.com/id/6638417/#.UgKCexbQ5UQ.

Hannerz, Ulf (1992), *Cultural Complexity*, New York: Columbia University Press.

Harrison, Bennet and Barry Bluestone (1990), The Great U-Turn: Corporate Restructuring and he Polarizing of America, New York: Basic Books.

Hebdige, Dick (1979), *Subculture: the Meaning of Style*, New York: Routledge.

Herskovitz, Stephen und Malcolm Crystal (2010), The Essential Brand Persona: Storytelling and Branding, *Journal of Business Strategy*, 31(3), 21–28.

Hill, Sam and Glenn Rifkin (1999), *Radical Marketing*, New York: Harper Business.

Holder, Stephen C. (1973), The Family Magazine and the American People, *Journal of Popular Culture*, 7 (2), 264–279.

Holt, Douglas B. (1997), Poststructuralist Lifestyle Analysis: Conceptualizing the Social Patterning of Consumption in Postmodernity, *Journal of Consumer Research,* 23, 326–350.

Holt, Douglas B. (2002), Why Do Brands Cause Trouble? A Dialectical Theory of Consumer Culture and Branding, *Journal of Consumer Research,* 29 (1), 70–90.

Holt, Douglas B. (2004), How Brands Become Icons: The Principles of Cultural Branding, Harvard: Harvard Business Press.

Holt, Douglas B. (2006a), Jack Daniel's America: Iconic Brands as Ideological Parasites and Proselytizers, *Journal of Consumer Culture, 6 (3),* 355–377.

Holt, Douglas B. (2006b), Toward a Sociology of Branding, *Journal of Consumer Culture,* 6, *299-302.*

Holt, Douglas B. and Douglas Cameron (2010), *Cultural Strategy: Using Innovative Ideologies to Build Breakthrough Brands*, Oxford: Oxford University Press.

Hirschman, Elizabeth C. (1988), The Ideology of Consumption: A Structural-Syntactical Analysis of "Dallas" and "Dynasty," *Journal of Consumer Research*, 15 (December), 344–359.

Hirschman, Elizabeth C. (1993), Ideology in Consumer Research—1980 and 1990: A Marxist and Feminist Critique, *Journal of Consumer Research,* 19 (March), 537–555.

Hirschman, Elizabeth C. and Craig J. Thompson (1997), Why Media Matter: Toward a Richer Understanding of Consumer's Relationships with Advertising and Mass Media, *Journal of Advertising,* 26 (1), 43–60.

Hirschman, Elizabeth C. and Morris B. Holbrook (1982), Hedonic Consumption: Emerging Concepts, Methods and Propositions, *Journal of Marketing,* 46 (Summer), 92–101.

Hyken, Shep (2009), The Cult of the Customer: Create an Amazing Customer Experience That Turns Satisfied Customers into Customer Evangelists, New Jersey: John Wiley & Sons.

Ideology (n.d.), in *Merriam Webster's online dictionary,* retrieved on August 12, 2013, from http://www.merriam-webster.com/dictionary/ideology.

Inglehart, Ronald and Wayne E. Baker (2000), Modernization, Cultural Change, and the Persistence of Traditional Values, *American Sociology Review,* 65 (1), 19–51.

Inglehart, Ronald (1997), Modernization and Postmodernization: Cultural, Economic, and Political Change in 43 Societies, Princeton: University Press.

Interbrand (2013), *Best Global Brands 2013,* retrieved on October 13, 2013, from http://www.interbrand.com/de/best-global-brands/2013/Best-Global-Brands-2013.aspx.

Isabella, Lynn A. (1990), Evolving Interpretations as a Change Unfolds: How Managers Construe Key Organizational Events, *The Academy of Management Journal,* 33 (1), 7–41.

Jankovich, Mark, Antonio Lazaro Reboll, Julian Stringer, and Any Willis (2003), *Defining Cult Movies: The Cultural Politics of Oppositional Taste*, Manchester: University Press.

Joy, Annamma and John F. Sherry, Jr. (2003), Speaking of Art as Embodied Imagination: A Multisensory Approach to Understanding Aesthetic Experience, *Journal of Consumer Research,* 30 (2), 259–282.

Kamakura, Wagner A. and Thomas P. Novak (1992), Value-System Segmentation: Exploring the Meaning of LOV, *Journal of Consumer Research,* 19 (1), 119–132.

Kates, Steven M. (2002), The Protean Quality of Subcultural Consumption: An Ethnographic Account of Gay Consumers, *Journal of Consumer Research,* 29 (December), 383–399.

Kiley, David (2002), Getting the Bugs Out: The Rise, Fall, and Comeback of Volkswagen in America, New York: Wiley.

Fournier, Susan (1998), Consumers and Their Brands: Developing Relationship Theory in Consumer Research, *Journal of Consumer Research,* 24 (March), 343–373.

Keller, Kevin L. (1993), Conceptualizing, Measuring and Managing Customer-Based Brand Equity, *Journal of Marketing,* 57, 1–22.

Keller, Kevin L. (1998), Branding Perspectives on Social Marketing, *in NA— Advances in Consumer Research Volume 25,* Joseph W. Alba and J. Wesley Hutchinson, eds., Provo, UT: Association for Consumer Research, 25, 299–302.

Kluckhohn, Clyde (1994), *Mirror for Man*, University of California.

Kozinets, Robert V. (2001), Utopian Enterprise: Articulating the Meaning of Star Trek's Culture of Consumption, *Journal of Consumer Research,* 28, 67–88.

Kozinets, Robert V. (2002), Can Consumers Escape the Market? Emancipatory Illuminations from Burning Man, *Journal of Consumer Research*, 29 (June), 20–38.

Kozinets, Robert V. and Jay M. Handelman (2004), Adversaries of Consumption: Consumer Movements, Activism, and Ideology, *Journal of Consumer Research,* 31 (3), 691–704.

Kravets, Olga and Örsan Örge (2010), Iconic Brands: A Socio-Material Story, *Journal of Material Culture,* 15 (2), 205–232.

Langone, Michael D. (1993), Recovery From Cults: Help for Victims of Psychological and Spiritual Abuse, New York: W.W. Norten.

Lesthaeghe, Ron (1983), A Century of Demographic and Cultural Change in Western Europe: An Exploration of Underlying Dimensions, *Population and Development Review*, 9 (3), 411–435.

Levy, Sidney J. (1959), Symbols for Sale, *Harvard Business Review,* 33 (March-April), 117–124.

Lois, George (2012), Damn Good Advice (for People with Talent)—How to Unleash Your Creative Potential by America's Master Communicator, London: Phaidon Press.

Matzler, Kurz, Elisabeth A. Pichler, and Andrea Hemetsberger (2007), *Who Is Spreading the Word? The Positive Influence of Extraversion on Consumer Passion and Brand Evangelism*, Paper presented at the AMA Winter Educator's Conference, Chicago: American Marketing Association.

McCracken, Grant (1986), Culture and Consumption: A Theoretical Account of the Structure and Movement of the Cultural Meaning of Consumer Goods, *Journal of Consumers Research,* 13 (June), 17–84.

McCracken, Grant (1987), Advertising: Meaning or Information, *Advances in Consumer Research*, 14, 121-124.

McCracken, Grant (1989), Who is the Celebrity Endorser? Cultural Foundations of the Endorsement Process, *Journal of Consumer Research,* 16 (3), 310–321.

McCracken, Grant (1990), Culture and Consumption, New Approaches to the Symbolic Character of Consumer Goods and Activities, Indiana: University Press.

McCracken, Grant (2012), Chief Culture Officer: How to Create a Living, Breathing Corporation, New York: Basic Books.

McKee, Robert (2003), Storytelling That Moves People, *Harvard Business Review,* 81 (6), 51–55.

Meserve, Harry C. (1979), Cult and Culture, *Journal of Religion and Health*, 18 (4), 255–259.

Meyerson, Rolf and Elihu Katz (1957), Notes on a Natural History of Fads, *American Journal of Sociology*, 62 (May), 594–601.

Miles, Matthew B. and A. Michael Huberman (1994), *Qualitative Data Analysis: An Expanded Sourcebook*, Beverly Hills, CA: Sage Publications.

Muñiz, Albert M., Jr. and Thomas C. O'Guinn (2001), Brand Community, *Journal of Consumer Research,* 27 (4), 412–432.

Myth (n.d.), in *Merriam Webster's online dictionary*, retrieved on September 26, 2013, from http://www.merriam-webster.com/dictionary/myth.

Nelson, Geoffrey K. (1968), The Concept of Cult, *Sociological Review,* 16, 351–362.

O'Brien, Kevin (2009, October 19), Nokia Tries to Undo Blunders in U.S., *The New York Times*, p. B4.

Our History (2013), The Body Shop Website, retrieved on July 12, 2013, from
http://www.thebodyshop.com/content/services/aboutus_history.aspx.

Patterson, Anthony und Stephen Brown (2005), No Tale, No Sale—A Novel
Approach to Marketing Communication, *The Marketing Review*, 5 (4),
315–328.

Park, C. Whan, Bernard J. Jaworski, and Deborah J. MacInnis (1986), Strategic
Brand Concept-Image Management, *The Journal of Marketing, 50,*
135–145.

Peng, Kaiping, Richard E. Nisbett, and Nancy Y. C. Wong (1997), Validity
Problems Comparing Values across Cultures and Possible Solutions,
Psychological Methods, 2 (April), 329–344.

Petersen, William J. (1982), *Those Curious New Cults in the 80s,* New Canaan:
Keats.

Phillips, Kevin (1993), Boiling Point: Democrats, Republicans, and the Decline of Middle-Class Prosperity, New York: Random House.

Pimentel, Ronald W. and Kristy E. Reynolds (2004), A Model for Consumer
Devotion: Affective Commitment with Proactive Sustaining Behaviors,
Academy of Marketing Science Review, 5, 1–45.

Ragas, Matthew W. and Bolivar J. Bueno (2002), The Power of Cult Branding:
How 9 Magnetic Brands Turned Customers into Loyal Follower, New
York: Crown Business.

Richins, Marsha L. (1994), Special Possessions and the Expression of Material
Values, *Journal of Consumer Research*, 21 (3), 522–533.

Rokeach, Milton (1973), *The Nature of Human Values*, New York: Free Press.

Rosman, Abraham, Paula G. Rubel, and Maxine Weisgrau (2009), *The Tapes-
try of Culture: An Introduction to Cultural Anthropology*, 9th Edition,
Plymouth: Altamira Press.

Rozanski, Horacio D., Allen G. Baum, and Bradley T. Wolfsen (1999), Brand Zealots: Realizing the Full Value of Emotional Brand Loyalty, *Strategy and Business,* 17, 51–62.

Schlanger, Danielle and Kim Bhasin (2012, June 25), 16 Brands That Have Fanatical Cult Followings, *Business Insider,* retrieved on October 14, 2013 from http://www.businessinsider.com/cult-brands-2012-6#.

Schouten, John W. and James H. McAlexander (1995), Subcultures of Consumption: An Ethnography of New Bikers, *Journal of Consumer Research*, 22 (1), 43–61.

Schroeder, Jonathan E. (2009), The Cultural Codes of Branding, *Marketing Theory*, 9 (1), 123–126.

Schultz, Howard and Joanne Gordon (2011), Onward: How Starbucks Fought for its Life without Losing its Soul, Rodale: New York.

Simmons, John (2006), Guinness and the Role of Strategic Storytelling, *Journal of Strategic Marketing*, 14, 11–18.

Sieber, Sam D. (1973), The Integration of Field Work and Survey Methods, *American Journal of Sociology*, 78 (May), 1335–1359.

Sherry, John F. (1995), Bottomless Cup, Plug-Drug: A Telethnography of Coffee, *Visual Anthropology*, 7 (4), 351–70.

Slotkin, Richard (1973), Regeneration Through Violence: The Mythology of the American Frontier, 1600-1860, Oklahoma: University Press.

Smeesters, Dirk, Thomas Mussweiler, and Naomi Mandel (2010), Should Advertisers Use Skinny Models? *RSM Insight—Management Knowledge,* 1st Quarter, 12–13.

Snyder, Charles Richard and Howard L. Fromkin (1980), *Uniqueness: The Human Pursuit of Difference*, New York: Plenium

Stark, Rodney and William S. Bainbridge (1985), *The Future of Religion: Secularization, Revival, and Cult Formation*, Berkeley, CA: University Press.

Strauss, Claudia and Naomi Quinn (1997), *A Cognitive Theory of Cultural Meaning*, Cambridge: University Press.

Subculture (n.d.) in Webster' s New World Dictionary of American English, online, retrieved on July 24, 2013, from http://www.merriam-webster.com/dictionary/subculture.

Taleb, Nassim N. (2012), *Antifragile: Things That Gain from Disorder*, New York: Random House.

Thompson, John B. (1984), *Studies in the Theory of Ideology*, California: University of California Press.

Thompson, Craig J. and Elizabeth C. Hirschman (1995), Understanding the Socialized Body: A Poststructuralist Analysis of Consumers' Self-Conceptions, Body Images, and Self-Care Practices, *Journal of Consumer Research*, 22 (2), 139–153.

Thompson, Craig J. and Diana L. Haytko (1997), Speaking of Fashion: Consumers' Use of Fashion Discourse and the Appropriation of Countervailing Cultural Meaning, *Journal of Consumer Research*, 24 (June), 15–42.

Thompson, Craig J. and Maura Troester (2002), Consumer Value Systems in the Age of Postmodern Fragmentation: The Case of the Natural Health Microculture, *Journal of Consumer Research,* 28 (4), 550–571.

Thompson, Craig J. and Zeynep Arsel (2004), The Starbucks Brandscape and Consumers' (Anticorporate) Experiences of Glocalization, *Journal of Consumer Research,* 31 (3), 631–642.

Thorton, Sarah (1997), General Introduction, in *The Subcultures Reader*, Ken Gelder and Sarah Thorton, eds., New York: Routledge.

Touraine, Alain (1981), *The Voice and the Eye*, Cambridge: Cambridge University Press.

Twitchell, James B. (2004), An English Teacher Looks at Branding, *Journal of Consumer Research*, 31, 484–489.

Wayland, Robert E. and Paul K. Cole (1997), *Customer Experience: New Strategies for Growth*, Cambridge: Harvard University Press.

Wells, Melanie (2001), Cult Brands, *Forbes,* 167 (9), 198–205.

Werdigier, Julia (2007, August 25), To Woo Europeans, McDonald's Goes Upscale, *The New York Times*, retrieve from http://www.nytimes.com/2007/08/25/business/worldbusiness/25restaurant.html.

Wiedmann, Klaus-Peter, Nadine Hennigs, Steffen Schmidt, and Thomas Wuestefeld (2011), Drivers and Outcomes of Brand Heritage: Consumers' Perception of Heritage Brands in the Automotive Industry, *Journal of Marketing Theory and Practice*, 19 (2), 205–220.

Williams, Raymond (1976), *Keywords*, New York: Oxford University Press.

Wilkinson, Sue (2003), Focus Groups, in *Qualitative Psychology: A Practical Guide to Research Methods*, Smith, J., ed., Beverly Hills: Sage Publications, 184–204.

Woodside, Arch G. (2010), Brand-Consumer Storytelling Theory and Research: Introduction to a Psychology & Marketing Special Issue, *Psychology & Marketing,* 27 (6), 531–540.

Woodside, Arch G., Suresh Sood und Kenneth E. Miller (2008), When Consumers and Brands Talk: Storytelling and Research in Psychology and Marketing, *Psychology & Marketing*, 25 (2), 97–145.

Yinger, Melton (1970), *The Scientific of Religion,* New York: McMillan.

Zaltman, Gerald (2003), *How Customers Think: Essential Insights into the Mind of Market*, Cambridge, MA: Harvard University Press.

PAPER 2

The Cult Brand Status Scale[5]

The phenomenon of cult brands is gaining increasing interest in brand management. This article describes six studies aimed at developing and validating a scale that measures the cult status of brands. Based on interdisciplinary conceptual considerations as well as qualitative interviews and focus groups, the authors identify six cult brand dimensions: (1) cultural-change orientation, (2) following, (3) pioneer, (4) richness of story, (5) persuasiveness, and (6) distinctiveness. The results of four large-scale quantitative studies show that the 24-item cult brand status scale (CBSS) is discriminant with regard to two measures—brand equity and brand likability. Moreover, cult brand status is influenced by brand experience and the hedonic nature of a brand and predicts consumers' word of mouth, brand attitude, and willingness to pay a price premium, particularly for consumers high in public self-consciousness, self-brand connection, and brand involvement.

---

[5] An earlier version of this paper has been successfully submitted and presented at the European Marketing Academy Conference, Lisbon, 2012. The authors intend to publish this paper to an international marketing journal in the current or in a modified version. It is based on a joint work with Lucia Malär, Bettina Nyffenegger, and Bianca Grohmann.

1   Introduction

The term *cult* is increasingly used to describe products and brands (VW Beetle, Gori 2001; Apple, Lindstrom 2011), movies (*The Big Lebowski*, Dean 2011; *Star Wars*, Holson 2005), and even people (Andy Warhol, Nunziata 2004). While the underlying phenomenon of cult brand status is not fully understood yet, there seems to be consensus that achieving cult brand status pays off (e.g., Apple, IKEA, Starbucks, and Harley-Davidson). "By employing a cult brand strategy, managers . . . can be sitting on top of a gold mine" (Carr 1996, p. 1). Among the most valuable global brands according to several annual rankings, quite a few brands are viewed as cult brands (Brady et al. 2004). Thus it comes as no surprise that the phenomenon of cult brands has attracted attention in marketing practice.

In a similar vein, cult brands have also been discussed in the academic (e.g., Acosta and Devasagayam 2010; Belk and Tumbat 2005; Holt 2004) and the managerial literature (e.g., Atkin 2004; Brady et al. 2004; Hyken 2009; Ragas and Bueno 2002). Based on qualitative interviews, case studies, and anecdotal evidence, this literature has contributed to our understanding of the phenomenon of cult brands. Both theory and practice, however, could benefit from a more elaborate conceptual discussion and empirical validation of the cult brand construct. Importantly, there seems to be some confusion about what constitutes cult brand status. For example, some authors simply equate cult brand status with strong brand performance (Brady et al. 2004), which may not capture the construct's essence. Cult brand status is a more complex concept than mere brand performance: "It's one thing to have people buy your products. It's another thing for them to tattoo your name on their bodies," a brand manager from Harley-Davidson was quoted (Palmer 2000, p. 90).

Against this background, our research further develops the

understanding of the cult brand phenomenon by conceptualizing cult brand status and by creating and validating a scale to measure the cult status of brands (i.e., the CBSS). Our interdisciplinary conceptualization embraces perspectives of religion, sociology, and psychology. In order to develop and validate the CBSS, we draw on findings of an extensive literature review, two qualitative studies based on four focus-group discussions with 29 participants, 54 individual in-depth interviews, 47 individual written reports, and four quantitative studies involving 5,190 consumers overall.

Our study aims at advancing the academic domain through a theoretically sound and empirically tested conceptualization that can be used in future brand management research. For those brand managers who strive to achieve cult brand status, a measurement instrument to assess progress toward this goal would be beneficial. Our research provides them with a tool to track and, therefore, increase their brands' cult status.

2   Conceptualizing the Dimensions of Cult Brand Status

Our conceptualization of cult brand status is derived from an interdisciplinary literature review, as well as a series of focus-group discussions and in-depth interviews (see the description of Study 1 for more details). A review of the literature has revealed various conceptualizations of the cult phenomenon in the fields of religious studies, sociology, and psychology.

In religious studies, the cult phenomenon is discussed in numerous conceptual papers that focus on such issues as the creation of cults, general characteristics of religious cults, and different types of cults (Campbell 1977; Ellwood 1986; Nelson 1969; Richardson 1993). General characteristics that appear in these conceptualizations are that religious cults (1) are collectives that follow specialized beliefs and practice certain rituals, (2) offer alternatives to the dominant spiritual tradition and culture, (3) are guided by charismatic leaders, (4) meet personal needs and are concerned with problems of individuals, and (5) provide powerful subjective experiences (Chalfant, Beckley, and Palmer 1986; Ellwood 1986; Melton and Moore 1982; Yinger 1970).

Sociology takes a perspective on cults that is similar to that of religious studies. More specifically, sociological studies take a closer look at the interaction of the cult with its host society (for an overview, see Dawson 2006). In this context, two key socioreligious processes are discussed: revival and innovation. While the revival of the original or pure spirit of the religious tradition is associated with sects, innovation is linked to the formation of cults (Bainbridge and Stark 1979; Stark and Bainbridge 1985). Hence, the creation of a cult signifies the introduction of an unconventional mode of religious expression that departs from tradition and culture (Lofland 1966; Pfautz 1955). More specifically, it is postulated that this ideological innovation is inspired by the outside predominant religious culture (Glock and Stark 1965; Richardson 1978) and often is motivated by dissatisfaction with the current state of society (Glock 1964). An additional conceptual consideration in sociology is that cults are often rather small spontaneous groups that lack formal organization and a definite authority structure (Richardson 1978). Furthermore, sociologists trans-fer the religious concept of a cult to more secular phenomena, such as cult movies. A typical cult movie questions "traditional authority structures, re-flects societal strains, and offers interpretable and paradoxical resolutions to these social strains" (Kinkade and Katovich 1992, p. 194).

Psychology also discusses the cult phenomenon. In addition to the ideas of religious and sociological studies, psychologists examine the role of the individual in the creation and practice of cults. In other words, an important unit of analysis here is the individual cult member, who devotes himself to some leader, ideal, or cult in general (Cantril and Sherif 1969). Further, psy-chologists examine the role and power of group leaders as well as their pro-gram of persuasion (Singer and Lalich 1995; Woody 2009). In this context, they further examine the individual motives and consequences of joining a cult—including negative consequences, such as excessive devotion, psycho-logical dependency, and thought-control (Langone 1993).

So far, in our literature review we have discussed the concept of cults from different perspectives and identified specific characteristics of a cult. As we integrate these characteristics in our conceptualization of cult brand status, it is important to note that we focus on the phenomenon of cult brands and not on the more general concept of cults. A cult and a cult brand differ with regard to the following aspects: While the members of religious cults follow a char-ismatic leader and show a strong devotion to religious rituals and objects, fol-lowers of secular cults focus on an object that guides transactions between them instead of a charismatic leader (Kinkade and Katovich 1992). The present research focuses on a secular cult in which a cult brand serves as the object of devotion and dedication of its followers (i.e., consumers). Our conceptualization of cult brand status intends to answer the following question: What characteristics should a brand possess in order to be the central object of a secular cult?

The literature on religious studies, sociology, psychology, the managerial literature, and insights from our qualitative interviews and focus-group discussions suggest that there are six dimensions that apply to secular cults and are central to cult brand status: cultural-change orientation, following, pioneer, richness of story, persuasiveness, and distinctiveness. We now discuss these six dimensions in more detail.

2.1   Cultural-Change Orientation

Cults respond to changes in the surrounding society or culture, are often characterized by deviant behavior, and tend to challenge existing structures, values, and beliefs (Bainbridge and Stark 1979; Stark and Bainbridge 1985). They frequently arise from small and individualized groups who follow and live new ideas (Bainbridge and Stark 1979; Campbell 1998; Nelson 1969; O'Dea 1968; Stark and Bainbridge 1985). An example for such a group is the hippie subculture that arose in the 1960s. When the dominant cultural values in the American society were rather "individualistic," the hippie subculture responded with "collectivistic" values (Richardson 1979). Such cultic responses can also arise in other areas of life—such as politics, sociology, medicine, economy, art, music, and movies (Richardson 1978). As an example, cult movies have a strong cultural orientation: they reflect cultural changes and societal strains within the dominant social structure and offer vanguard resolutions (Kinkade and Katovich 1992).

In a branding context, a brand that focuses its product on relevant cultural and societal changes (e.g., changes in lifestyle, mobility, eating habits) is prone to become the object of a cult and hence to have a high cult status. Such cultural and societal changes often have origin in subcultures new to the surrounding society (Dawson 2006). One of our interviewees confirmed this by stating, "Nike at first has been well-known and worn in the subculture of athletic immigrants." Nike picked up on societal strains such as social discrimination, racism, and sexism, which were emergent societal discourses in the late 1970s, and created a novel ideology saying that challenges have nothing to do with barriers such as racism or poverty, but with solo-willpower (Holt and Cameron 2010). Nike developed its communication around the idea of willpower. It abandoned classical celebrity endorsement and used mainstream people instead. They communicated the brand ideology through the well-known slogan "Just Do It." Two other examples are the Volkswagen Beetle and Starbucks. At a time when cars served as a status symbol, Volkswagen challenged this function by creating the "live below your means" ideology and launched the Volkswagen Beetle. The ads depicted real Beetle owners without reference to luxury attributes but rather focused on the small and affordable Beetle. By doing so, the Beetle appealed to the growing subculture of people with alternative lifestyles and less materialistic values such as artists and hippies (Holt 2004).

Starbucks capitalized on a need for a more sophisticated lifestyle, driven by higher education levels and exposure to other cultures, which arose in the 1980s. Starbucks picked up on this cultural change and started offering high-quality coffee—providing consumers with a taste of luxury at an affordable price. "Starbucks just built a world around coffee and turned it into something special," one of our interviewees said. By reflecting this cultural change in lifestyle, Starbucks laid the ground for its cult brand status (Holt and Cameron 2010).

Based on these conceptual considerations we define the dimension *cultural-change orientation* as the degree to which a brand's creation is based on societal and cultural changes.

2.2   Following

A defining characteristic of cults is the existence of a highly devoted following (Chalfant, Beckley, and Palmer 1986; Langone 1993). Such followers collectively share specialized beliefs and are characterized by a strong emotional attachment and a dedicated loyalty to the cult. The followers' devotion to the cult can be explained as follows: the cult can fulfill the followers' social needs of belonging to a group of like-minded people, as the cult offers a bonded community of cult members with mutual problems, similar needs, and congruent desires (Stark and Bainbridge 1985).

The existence of a devoted following is also highly relevant in the context of cult brands: in the managerial literature on cult branding, highly emotional and loyal consumers who worship the brand are viewed as one of the essential characteristics of cult brands (Atkin 2004). Devoted cult followers know the brand more than anyone else, have the power to influence prospective customers, and defend the brand with the right arguments (Wells 2001). The followers' bonds toward the cult brand are usually so strong that cult brands become part of their lives (Acosta and Devasagayam 2010). Cult brand followers jointly create group thinking characterized by shared experiences and a strong feeling of belonging and of being similar to other group members (Acosta and Devasagayam 2010; McAlexander, Schouten, and Koenig 2002; Muñiz and Schau 2005).

On the basis of this conceptual discussion, we define the cult brand status dimension of following as the strength of the bond connecting the brand to its followers. This bond is characterized by worshiping and a sense of belonging.

2.3   Pioneer

A cult's ideology often departs significantly from the prevailing belief of the surrounding culture and is therefore progressive. It thus sets new trends for the society and takes a pioneer role (Atkin 2004). Such pioneering is based on innovation (Bainbridge and Stark 1979) and new knowledge (Dawson 2006) or even thought-reform programs (Langone 1993).

Also in the context of cult branding, pioneering plays a key role. Cult brands set new trends by offering innovative benefits and by doing so, inspire consumers and thus are pioneers (Holt and Cameron 2010). One of our interviewees said this: "A cult brand is not a fad. A cult brand is like a revolution. It creates something totally new that inspires others, other consumers, and other brands." Another respondent stated, "I see Apple as a real cult brand. By introducing the iPhone, Apple not only completely changed the importance, and usefulness of cell phones, but also the way people use them." Similarly, one interviewee stated, "EasyJet was one of the first airlines offering low-budget flights. With this new idea it revolutionized the aviation industry in Europe."

The key characteristic of a pioneer is important not only at the emergence of a new cult brand but also at later stages of its lifecycle, when the cult brand has to continuously reinvent itself to maintain a competitive advantage over imitators. A prominent example of damage to the cult status of a brand due to a lack in dynamism and pioneering spirit is the cell phone company Nokia. A key prerequisite for achieving innovativeness and pioneer capabilities is certainly a high level of creativity (Ragas and Bueno 2002). Only brands that are perceived as offering creative solutions to deprivation and other cultural tensions achieve the required pioneer authority that characterizes cult brands. An interviewee said: "Nokia once set trends for the entire cell phone industry . . . they just missed staying on the ball and got overtaken by more innovative suppliers." In contrast, by introducing the iPod, Apple changed the way people listen to music, and Apple's launch of the iPhone revolutionized the idea of a cell phone.

Based on this discussion, we define the *pioneer* dimension of cult brand status as the degree to which a brand takes a pioneer role by offering innovative benefits and creating new standards, values, and meaning systems in a changing environment.

2.4   Richness of Story

At the center of most cults there is a sacred text or narrative (Graeme 2007). These narratives include specific stories to illustrate the cult's key ideas and often refer to the story of the cult's origins and its founder or leader (e.g., Swallow 1982). Cults tend to see themselves as legitimated by a long tradition of wisdom or practice of which they are the current manifestation (Ellwood 1986).

This narrative element also plays an important role in a cult-branding context. Cult brands often have a rich, memorable, and inspiring story. Cult brand stories frequently relate to the foundation of the brand, its traditions, its conflicts and struggles (to create a rallying point), its triumph and tragedy (to humanize the brand), its creation (to emphasize the quality of the product and the management), its history and heritage, its location, its community, its consumers, or its products (Beverland 2009).

The followers of a cult brand are eager to get to know context stories about the brand, its origin, and history. Followers even share stories about the brand with others (Douglas and Ishwerwood 1979; Holt 2004). Stories are important because followers derive value from identifying themselves with stories and people (Holt 2004). For example, one of our interviewees explained her passion for Louis Vuitton: "It is especially the legendary history of Louis Vuitton that fascinates me about this brand. The master craftsman Louis Vuitton himself invented elegant bags for the French elite travelers of the 19th century. I love my Louis Vuitton Noe handbag, which was designed to carry four bottles of champagne."

Numerous brands refer to their rich history and their long tradition in their storytelling activities (Holt 2004) and even mythologize these stories (Atkin 2004; Beverland 2009) in order to increase the brand's cult status. Apple, for example, is a brand that understands the power of storytelling (Belk and Tumbat 2005). The cult of Macintosh is based on a creation myth, a hero myth, and a resurrection myth. The creation myth refers to Steve Jobs and Stephen Wozniak creating a computer in Steve's garage. The hero myth consists of the call to adventure, a helper, a journey, trials, culminating in a resurrection (i.e., a comeback) and a boon that restores the world (Belk and Tumbat 2005).

We define the cult brand status dimension of *richness of story* as the brand's ability to convey a special and long history to its consumers, who share the narrative content among each other.

2.5   Persuasiveness

The cult's persuasion potential is a key driver of cult creation (Singer and Lalich 1995): individuals need to be persuaded about the cult's central beliefs and messages—through the cult's and the cult leader's tactics and behaviors (e.g., Keiser and Keiser 1987; Singer and Lalich 1995; West 1989)—in order to be converted to loyal cult followers. The psychology and sociology literature extensively discusses the general underlying dynamics of persuasion (for an overview, see Perloff 2010): the persuasiveness of the message source (i.e., sender) has been identified as a key driver of persuasion. Factors that tend to increase the source's persuasiveness—and therefore the likelihood of persuasion—are credibility (Petty and Wegener 1998) and trustworthiness (McGinnis and Ward 1980) of the message source.

In the context of cult brands, persuasiveness is a key characteristic of a cult brand. The persuasion literature and findings of our qualitative interviews suggest that consumers perceive a brand as highly persuasive, not only based on its trustworthiness, credibility, honesty, and genuineness, but also based on superior performance or quality (Atkin 2004; Beverland 2009). For example, an interviewee noted, "I think that Apple is a cult brand because it has higher quality and warranty. It represents great advance in technology and it is a credible brand that you can trust." In a similar vein, one of the interviewees stated, "In my view, this brand is just true to itself and to its customers and therefore genuine. This brand doesn't need to pretend something that it's not. The brand promises high quality and this is what you really get."

The cult brand status dimension of *persuasiveness* is defined as the brand's potential to convincingly convey its key beliefs and messages based on authenticity and superior performance.

2.6   Distinctiveness

A cult presents a distinct alternative to dominant patterns within the society, so its ideology departs significantly from the prevailing beliefs of the surrounding culture (Bainbridge and Stark 1979; Ellwood 1986). The creation of a cult signifies the introduction of an unconventional mode of religious expression that departs from tradition and culture (Lofland 1966; Pfautz 1955). Thus a cult offers its followers the opportunity to differentiate themselves from other people (Whitsett 1992). The notion of distinctiveness has also been discussed in the context of secular cults. Cult movies, for example, offer novel resolutions, distinctive points of view, and alternative solutions to societal strains. They distinguish themselves from the mainstream and generally make a statement against accepted beliefs. Cult movies often are in opposition to standard Hollywood schemata and mainstream tastes (Kinkade and Katovich 1992).

In the context of cult brands, distinctiveness is also highly relevant. According to the cult brand literature, cult brands define a distinct ideology and differentiate themselves based on a unique identity (Holt 2004; Holt and Cameron 2010; Ragas and Bueno 2002). They achieve significant distinction in terms of functionality (e.g., Swiss Army knife), design (e.g., Ray-Ban), communication (e.g., Coca-Cola), and emotional relevance (e.g., Tiffany &

Co.) to escape direct competition with mainstream brands. It has been argued that such distinctiveness can even evoke the sacred character of a brand (Belk, Wallendorf, and Sherry 1989). Examples of brands that successfully created unique and distinctive brand associations that contribute to their cult status are Nespresso (sensuality), Red Bull (overcoming challenges), and Vespa (la dolce vita—the Italian good life). A participant pointed out that "the unique roaring and the feeling of aggressive power is what makes a Ferrari so special."

Based on this discussion, we define the cult brand status dimension of *distinctiveness* as the brand's ability to position itself as significantly different from competitive brands based on easily recognizable characteristics.

3   Cult Brand Status and Related Concepts

The concept of cult brand status distinguishes itself from several other related concepts: brand personality (Aaker 1997), brand love (Batra, Ahuvia, and Bagozzi 2011), brand attachment (Park et al. 2010), brand community (McAlexander, Schouten, and Koenig 2002; Muñiz and Schau 2005), subcultures of consumption (Schouten and McAlexander 1995), cultural branding and iconicity (Holt 2004; Holt and Cameron 2010), and sacred and profane consumption (Belk, Wallendorf, and Sherry 1989).

Brand personality (Aaker 1997) relates to person-like characteristics that describe a brand. While some brand personality dimensions are similar to cult brand status dimensions (e.g., excitement and pioneer), cult brand status additionally captures a brand's cultural-change orientation, richness of story, and following. Brand love (Batra, Ahuvia, and Bagozzi 2011) and brand attachment (Park et al. 2010) both relate to the emotional branding paradigm that postulates that an important aspect of a brand is to build strong emotion-based relationships with consumers (see also Holt 2004). While these emotion-based relationships certainly describe some forms of relations consumers have with brands, cult brand status focuses on the characteristics of a brand that are indicative of its cult status among consumers, such as perceived richness of story and distinctiveness. The central focus of the construct of brand community (McAlexander, Schouten, and Koenig 2002; Muñiz and Schau 2005) and subcultures of consumption (Schouten and McAlexander 1995) is on how groups of consumers relate to a brand and to each other and, hence is somehow related to the following dimension. However, cult brand status is a more comprehensive concept that captures how brands resolve important tensions in consumers' lives by offering new solutions, which is reflected in the dimensions of cultural-change orientation, pioneer, and distinctiveness.

Cult brand status also relates to iconicity within a cultural branding paradigm (Holt 2004; Holt and Cameron 2010). However, it broadens the cultural branding paradigm's focus on culture and myth. In addition, cult brand status relates to some extent to the literature on sacred and profane consumption (Belk, Wallendorf, and Sherry 1989), which first raised the possibility that objects and products can become sacred from a consumer's perspective. However, the current conceptualization extends this notion specifically to the domain of brands and offers a description of cult brand characteristics that characterize brands worthy of worship.

Overall, each dimension of cult brand status relates to some extent to existing branding and marketing constructs. Their combination, however, reflects a previously unmeasured phenomenon that captures the cult status of a brand.

4 Scale Construction and Validation

In order to develop and validate the CBSS we draw on two qualitative and four quantitative studies. Study 1 is a qualitative study with the purpose to generate a broad base of potential scale items. In our second qualitative study, consumers described cult brands and noncult brands, which allowed us to capture consumers' understanding of cult brands. Study 3 is the initial scale administration. A further study then applies the refined 24-item CBSS to different cult and noncult brands in Europe and North America. In Study 5, we establish discriminant validity of the overall scale with regard to brand equity and brand likability, as well as dimension-level discriminant validity with regard to several related constructs. The final study establishes nomological validity: we examine drivers of cult brand status perceptions, the outcomes of such perceptions, as well as moderating variables.

4.1 Study 1: Item Generation

The generation of items for the six cult brand dimensions was based on an extensive literature search, as well as 54 30-minute in-depth interviews with consumers who recently had bought a brand that we considered to be a cult brand and four semistructured focus-group discussions that took on average two hours. Focus group 1 consisted of six university professors of theology, anthropology, sociology, psychology, philosophy of culture, and political science. Focus group 2 consisted of eight professionals from the fields of secondary education, medicine, communications, military, management, and consulting. Focus group 3 (seven participants) consisted of artists in music and fashion as well as athletes. Focus group 4 consisted of eight fans of musicians, sports teams, cars, and technology.

In combination with our literature review, these in-depth interviews and focus-group discussions led to 319 items that capture the cult brand status. Based on expert ratings provided by five marketing academics from different universities and business schools, items were eliminated if at least one expert believed that it was ambiguous or a poor representation of the construct, or if only two out of the five experts rated it as fair. This procedure resulted in 127 items.

4.2   Study 2: Consumers' Conceptions of Cult Brands

For further validation of our cult brand dimensions, we considered consumers' understanding of what a cult brand is. In an exploratory study, we asked graduate business students ($n = 47$, 42.6% female, Median age = 24 years) to think about cult brands in general, to identify a brand with high cult status, and to describe why they thought the brand had high cult status. In a second step, we asked participants to choose a brand with relatively low cult status in the same or a related category and to describe their perception of the brand. We did not provide any other instructions, such that participants relied on their own understanding of a cult brand status to complete the task.

After one hour, every participant provided us with on average two pages of a written description of both a cult brand and a noncult brand. They described brands with high cult status such as shown in Figure 5.

Figure 5: Brands with High Cult Status

They also described brands with low cult status as illustrated in Figure 6.

Figure 6: Brands with Low Cult Status

Our content analysis of all the open-ended responses revealed that all respondents had in their mind a concept of cult brand. The participants provided descriptions of cultural change orientation (e.g., "it really understands what people want," "they want to be part of an urban culture," and "it breaks the general way of thinking"), pioneer (e.g., "trendy," "innovative," and "reinventing"), following (e.g., "it has its own fandom," "they want to be part of a certain lifestyle," and "brand is worshiped and lived by its costumers"), richness of story (e.g., "it has a long history," "it is well-known over generations"), persuasiveness (e.g., "honest," "credible," and "superior product"), and distinctiveness (e.g., "distinct from other brands," "unique," "individual," and "recognized"). As participants also described brands with low cult status, we analyzed these descriptions and categorized them according to the six cult brand status dimensions. The descriptions of brands with a low cult status (i.e., noncult brands) mostly appeared as contradiction to our dimensions such as "just another product" or "not liked in society" and "not standing for a certain lifestyle" (for cultural-change orientation); "tries to imitate brand X," "copies trends, others set" (for pioneer); "no one will remember this brand two years from now," "it is not conveying any emotions," "there's nothing behind it," and "meaningless" (for richness of story); "profit-oriented," "short-termed," and "not superior among competitors," (for persuasiveness); "not creative or not new to me," "just average," and "does not come up with something really new" (for distinctiveness). Overall, this study shows that our conceptualization of cult brands reflects consumers' conceptions of cult brands, which also arose in the focus groups and in the in-depth interviews.

4.3   Study 3: Initial Administration

In Study 3, 569 consumers in Europe (46.4% female, Median age = 25 years) used 127 items (on seven-point scales anchored by *not at all descriptive* and *extremely descriptive*) to rate one of ten well-known brands representing four product classes (fast-moving consumer goods, durable consumer goods, services, and retail) in an online study. A pretest ($n = 47$) suggested inclusion of the cult brands Apple, Harley-Davidson, IKEA, Red Bull, and Starbucks and the noncult brands Charles Vögele, Nissan, Philips, Switcher, and UPC Cable-com. The respondent was only allowed to continue with the corresponding brand if he indicated a brand familiarity of at least 5 (7 = *maximum familiarity*;

1 = *no familiarity*). If the respondent indicated a brand familiarity below 5, a new brand was randomly assigned until the person's brand familiarity was 5 or higher.

In a principal components exploratory factor analysis, a seven-factor solution with 46 items emerged after the exclusion of cross-loading items. A confirmatory factor analysis (CFA; AMOS 20) led to item elimination based on individual item reliabilities (<.50), resulting in a six-factor structure with 24 items in total: cultural-change orientation (3 items), following (3 items), pioneer (5 items), richness of story (3 items), persuasiveness (7 items), and distinctiveness (3 items). The six-factor model had acceptable fit values ($\chi2/df$ = 4.33; NFI = .89; NNFI = .90; CFI = .91; SRMR = .07; RMSEA = .08). The average variance extracted (AVE; Fornell and Larcker 1981) for all factors was greater than .51, suggesting that all factors are unidimensional (AVE: cultural change orientation = .61; following = .67; pioneer = .68; richness of story = .51; persuasiveness = .63; distinctiveness = .62; see Appendix for a summary of all scale characteristics). Discriminant validity (Fornell and Larcker 1981) was supported with AVE for all factors exceeding squared correlations between all pairs of constructs. A second-order factor model (i.e., six factors load on a higher-order factor that represents the cult status of a brand) showed an acceptable fit ($\chi2/df$ = 4.79; NFI = .87; NNFI = .88; CFI = .90; SRMR = .08; RMSEA = .08). With one exception, indicator reliabilities exceeded .40 (cultural change orientation = .50; following = .61; pioneer = .69; richness of story = .38; persuasiveness = .45; distinctiveness = .62). Composite reliability of the higher-order factor was .87 and AVE was .54. The six dimensions thus capture the higher-order construct cult brand status.

4.4   Study 4a: Scale Generalizability among European Consumers

The aim of this study was to show that the CBSS captures the perceived cult status of a brand. Furthermore we wanted to test the scale's generalizability by employing new brands and a new sample of participants.

4.4.1 Pretest

In this study, we included brands high in cult status used in Study 3 (Apple, Harley-Davidson, IKEA, and Starbucks) and new brands based on our prior pretest (see Study 2) and the focus-group discussions. We chose Burton, Converse, easyJet, Facebook, Freitag, Havaianas, Migros, Red Bull, Tiffany & Co., and Vespa as brands high in cult status. Bata, bing.com, Conforama, Diadora, Fossil, Granini, McCafé, RBS, Seat, Spar, and TomTailor served as brands lower in cult status.

4.4.2 Design, Sample, and Procedure

In a within-participants online study, 622 European consumers (51 % female; Median age = 24 years) were randomly assigned to one of the fourteen cult brands as well as to one of the eleven non-cult brands (the same brand familiarity filtering procedure was applied as in Study 3). They rated the brands on the 24-item CBSS and completed a six-item product category expertise ($\alpha = .91$), and a three-item brand knowledge scale ($\alpha = .81$). Respondents further rated their familiarity with the brand (single item; mean = 6.35 on a seven-point scale) and provided demographic information.

4.4.3 Results

An Amos 20 measurement model of the 24-item CBSS showed good model fit (χ^2/df = 7.20; *NFI* = .92; *NNFI* = .92; *CFI* = .93; *SRMR* = .05; *RMSEA* = .07). Factor loadings of all items exceeded .81 and the corrected item-to-total correlations were greater than .59. *AVE* exceeded .55 and composite reliabilities of the scale exceeded .79. Cronbach's α values were generally high (cultural change orientation, α = .85; following, α = .82; pioneer, α = .94; richness of story, α = .78; persuasiveness, α = .94; distinctiveness, α = .81).

4.4.4 Discussion

This second administration of the CBSS to a new set of brands demonstrates the scale's generalizability. Results also suggest that the scale is applicable to a variety of brands of different categories.

4.5 Study 4b: Scale Generalizabilty among North American Consumers

The objective of this study was to test the psychometric properties of the CBSS in a different market context with a modified set of brands.

4.5.1 Pretest

The brands selected for this study consisted in part of brands used in other validation studies (Starbucks, Harley-Davidson) as well as a set of new brands that were unique to the North American context in which this study was carried out (Tim Hortons and McCafé coffee shops, Canada Goose jackets,

Wal-Mart stores, No Name, and President's Choice private label grocery items). This new set of brands was identified by means of a pretest in which 40 participants (60% female, Median age = 21 years) listed cult brands and noncult brands that came to their mind.

4.5.2 Design, Sample, and Procedure

In a one-factor between-participants study, 473 North American consumers recruited through an online panel (48.6% female, Median age = 53 years) rated one of the eight brands on the 24-item CBSS, completed a single-item brand familiarity, a six-item product category expertise ($\alpha = .94$) and a three-item brand knowledge scale ($\alpha = .88$) and provided demographic information. We applied the same brand familiarity filtering procedure as in Study 3.

4.5.3 Results

In a measurement model (Amos 20) involving the six correlated dimensions of the 24-item CBSS (cultural-change orientation, $\alpha = .93$; following, $\alpha = .92$; pioneer, $\alpha = .96$; richness of story, $\alpha = .9$; persuasiveness, $\alpha = .97$; distinctiveness, $\alpha = .89$), all items had factor loadings exceeding .66 and corrected item-to-total correlations exceeding .69. The model showed adequate fit with $\chi^2/df = 4.21$, *NFI* = .92, *NNFI* = .93, *CFI* = .94, *RMSEA* = .08, and *SRMR* = .05. The composite reliabilities exceeded .88 and AVE exceeded .53 for all dimensions. Average variance extracted (Fornell and Larcker 1981) suggested discriminant validity among the six dimensions.

4.5.4 Discussion

This study confirmed the psychometric properties of the CBS scale with a different set of brands. In this administration to a new sample, the scale achieved good model fit and reliability.

4.6   Study 5: Discriminant Validity

In Study 5, we examined the degree to which the proposed CBSS assesses the cult brand status and not other constructs (i.e., *discriminant validity*; Churchill 1979). The aim of this study was to establish discriminant validity of the overall CBSS and its dimensions with regard to relevant and conceptually related marketing measures.

4.6.1 Sample, Procedure, and Measures

In an online survey, 480 consumers (46.5% female, Median age = 25 years) rated one randomly assigned brand (the same brand familiarity filtering procedure was applied as in Study 3). For this study, we selected fifteen brands based on the Interbrand's ranking of the best global brands 2011—some brands with rather high cult status (Apple, Coca-Cola, Harley-Davidson, IKEA, Nike, Nivea, and Starbucks) and some with lower cult status (AXA, Colgate, Credit Suisse, H&M, Kellogg's, Microsoft, Nissan, Nokia, and Philips) based on pretest results.

4.6.2 Discriminant Validity of the Overall CBSS

In a first step, we provide evidence for discriminant validity of our overall measure of cult brand status (i.e., higher-order factor). Cult status is often associated with high brand performance (e.g., Brady et al. 2004). A widely used measure to assess a brand's performance is brand equity, which refers to the value added to a product by its brand name (e.g., Keller 1993; Park and Srinivasan 1994). Although brand equity and cult brand status reflect distinct theoretical concepts, it appears that the two measures relate to each other. We assessed brand equity in two ways. First, participants rated brand equity on a four-item scale (Yoo, Donthu, and Lee 2000). Second, we considered the Interbrand's brand value of 2011 (in $m) as a measure of brand equity based on secondary data.

The CBSS displayed discriminant validity with regard to both brand equity measures. Based on the criterion of Fornell and Larcker (1981), the AVE of brand equity (.84) exceeded the squared correlation between the two constructs (.28), which suggests that overall, CBS is discriminant with regard to brand equity. Since the AVE could not be computed for the brand values of Interbrand (i.e., single-item), we assessed the discriminant validity on the basis of a chi-square difference test (Anderson and Gerbing 1993; Homburg and Dobratz 1992), where the chi-square value of a restricted model in which cult brand status and brand equity are constrained to be perfectly correlated is compared with the chi-square value of an unrestricted model in which the correlation between the two constructs is different from one (i.e., the two constructs are distinct). Since the restricted model showed a significantly poorer fit than the unrestricted model ($\Delta\chi^2 = 5.69$, $\Delta df = 1$; $p < .05$) and the correlation between cult brand status and the Interbrand's brand equity measure was low (.16), cult brand status is discriminant from brand equity.

Another construct that is conceptually related to cult brand status is brand likability in a product category, which reflects the extent to which brands in a specific category are seen as interesting and worth spending time with (Keller 2001). Brand likability is an important facet of *brand knowledge* and *brand image* (Keller 1993) and reflects consumers' predisposition toward brands and the overall role of brands in customers' decision making in a specific category (Fischer, Völckner, and Sattler 2010). While one could argue that in some product categories cult brands are more likely to arise and hence cult brand status should be similar to brand likability, we believe that cult brand status reflects a multifaceted construct that refers to brands independent of the category. Brand likability was measured with two items from Fischer, Völckner, and Sattler (2010). The results showed that brand likability is clearly discriminant from our CBSS. AVE of brand likability (.74) exceeded the squared correlation between the two constructs (.19).

4.6.3 Discriminant Validity of the Single CBSS Dimensions

We also established discriminant validity on the dimensional level of the CBSS and analyzed the association between each of the six cult brand status dimensions and several related constructs. First, discriminant validity between cultural-change orientation and customer orientation was examined. To assess customer orientation, we used six items of the market orientation scale (Narver and Slater 1999) that measure customer orientation. Second, following was compared with brand loyalty (3 items; Yoo, Donthu, and Lee 2000), brand loyalty intention (4 items; Yoo and Donthu 2001), brand fans (3 items; Wakefield and Barnes 1996), and brand community interest (3 items; McAlexander, Schouten, and Koenig 2002). Third, richness of story was compared with the construct nostalgic connection (5 items; Fournier 1994). Fourth, we examined discriminant validity between persuasiveness and perceived brand quality (5 items based on Yoo, Donthu, and Lee 2000). Fifth, we compared distinctive-ness with perceived brand differentiation (4 items; Netemeyer et al. 2004) and brand clarity (3 items; slightly adapted from Fischer, Völckner, and Sattler 2010). Finally, pioneer was compared to the brand personality dimension ex-citement (11 items; Aaker 1997). With one exception (pioneer compared with excitement), we obtained evidence of discriminant validity for all cult brand status dimensions: AVE exceeded the squared correlation between the con-structs (Fornell and Larcker 1981). Table 3 reports the results of the discrimi-nant validity tests. We could not establish discriminant validity between the cult dimension pioneer and the brand personality dimension excitement, most likely because of the conceptual overlap of these two constructs and the result-ant overlap in scale items.

4.6.4 Discussion

Overall, the results suggest that the CBSS is related to, but distinct from other brand measures. Our dimensions and the overall CBSS show discriminant validity with regard to other conceptually related constructs in marketing.

Related Construct	Coeffic- ient Alpha	Composite Reliability	AVE	Squared Correlation With CBS or Respective Dimension
Brand Equity	0.95	0.95	0.84	.28 (with overall CBS)
Brand Equity (Interbrand)	---	---	---	.03 (with overall CBS)
Brand Like-ability	0.84	0.85	0.74	.19 (with overall CBS)
Customer Orientation	0.87	0.87	0.54	.23 (with cultural-change orientation)
Brand Loyalty	0.9	0.9	0.76	.12 (with following)
Brand Loyalty Intention	0.89	0.89	0.68	.12 (with following)
Brand Fans	0.89	0.89	0.72	.18 (with following)
Brand Commu-nity Interest	0.79	0.79	0.55	.12 (with following)
Nostalgic Connection	0.87	0.87	0.58	.09 (with richness of story)
Brand Quality	0.92	0.92	0.7	.47 (with persuasiveness)
Brand Differentiation	0.93	0.93	0.76	.39 (with distinctiveness)
Brand Clarity	0.89	0.89	0.74	.23 (with distinctiveness)
Excitement	0.86	0.86	0.52	.68 (with pioneer)

Table 3: Discriminant Validity Tests of the CBSS and its Dimensions

4.7   Study 6: Nomological Validity

This study applied the CBSS to examine the drivers of a brand's cult status and the impact of cult brand status on brand-related consumer responses, as well as several consumer-related moderating variables. The conceptual model of this nomological validity test is illustrated in Figure 7. We first discuss the drivers and then the outcomes of cult brand status. Subsequently, we postulate three moderating variables of the relationship between cult brand status and its outcomes.

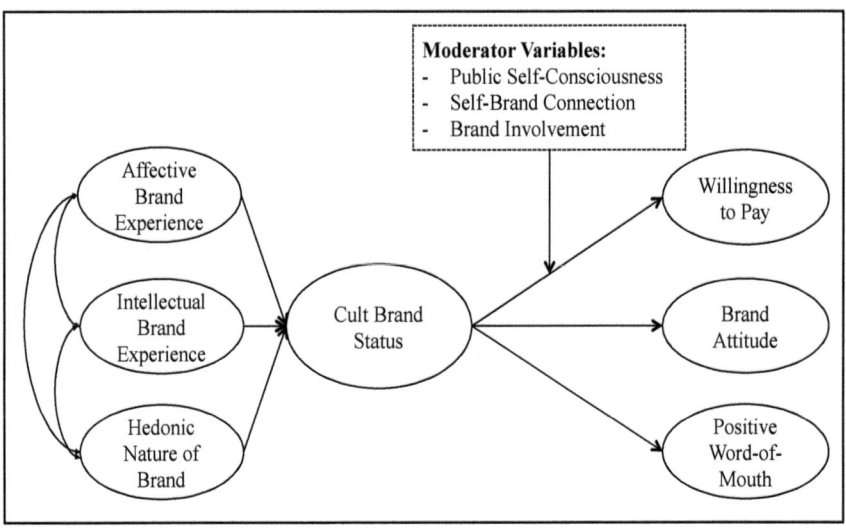

Figure 7: Conceptual Framework Nomological Validity

4.7.1 Antecedents of Cult Brand Status

A first potential antecedent of a brand's cult status is brand experience. Brand experience is conceptualized as "subjective, internal consumer responses (sensations, feelings, and cognitions) and behavioral responses evoked by brand-related stimuli that are part of a brand's design and identity, packaging, communications, and environments" (Brakus, Schmitt, and Zarantonello 2009, p. 53). Since experiences are used as information about a particular object (Pham 2004), the judgment about a brand's cult status may be related to a consumer's specific brand experiences. We argue that there are particularly two dimensions of brand experience that drive a brand's cult status: the affective and the intellectual brand experience. The former includes feelings generated by the brand; the latter refers to the ability of the brand to stimulate consumers' curiosity and engage them in convergent and divergent thinking (Zarantonello and Schmitt 2010). A brand's cult status comprises various dimensions, which consumers evaluate based on their experiences with the brand. To judge whether a brand orients itself toward culture and has a novel ideology, consumers may rely on their intellectual experiences with that brand. For example, consumers' impression that Southwest Airlines has a novel ideology by offering low-budget flights might rely on their experience on how the brand stimulated their curiosity and solved their problems. In a similar vein, affective experiences with a brand may increase the perception of several cult dimensions such as distinctiveness and following. For example, the emotional experiences that Harley-Davidson bikers share when driving on Route 66 may strengthen consumers' belief that Harley-Davidson has religious followers.

Hence, we expect the following:

H1a: **The affective and intellectual dimensions of brand experience positively relate to a brand's cult status.**

We also expect hedonic benefits of a brand to play an important role in the development of cult brand status. Hedonic benefits are multisensory and associated with enjoyment, fun, feelings, pleasure, and excitement (Chitturi, Raghunathan, and Mahajan 2007; Hirschman and Holbrook 1982). Hedonic brands tend to generate strong emotional responses (Hirschman and Holbrook 1982), are experientially appealing (Okada 2005), and delight consumers, rather than merely satisfy them (Chitturi, Raghunathan, and Mahajan 2008). Benefits such as enjoyment, excitement, and fun may increase overall cult brand perceptions by positively affecting several cult brand dimensions such as following and richness of story. Based on these considerations, we hypothesize the following:

H1b: **The hedonic nature of a brand positively relates to a brand's cult status.**

4.7.2 Consequences of Cult Brand Status

A brand's cult status provides consumers with benefits and hence increases the perceived value of the brand for the consumer along several dimensions. First, functional value primarily results from a cult brand's persuasiveness. By providing high quality products, having proven itself, and being a credible and genuine brand, a cult brand provides functional benefits to its consumers. Second, emotional value results from a cult brand's distinctiveness, richness of story, and pioneer. By having a special story and a long history, by setting trends, and by being creative and distinct from other brands, a cult brand provides emotional benefits to consumers. Third, social value results from consumers' devotion to a brand (e.g., resulting in a sense of belonging) and cultural change orientation (e.g., by responding to emerging needs in society).

Because cult status provides functional, emotional, and social value to consumers, we expect that the stronger a brand's cult status, the more favorable consumers' responses to that brand will be. We examine three brand-related consumer responses that should be positively affected: willingness to pay a price premium, brand attitude, and positive word of mouth.

First, willingness to pay a price premium is defined as the excess price a consumer is willing to pay for a brand over comparable products or brands (Netemeyer et al. 2004) and is based on the extent consumers associate value with a brand (Park and Srinivasan 1994). The link between perceived value and willingness to pay a price premium has been established in several prior studies (e.g., Homburg, Koschate, and Hoyer 2005). Since a brand with a high cult status offers functional, emotional, and social value to consumers, we expect that consumers are willing to pay a higher price for these benefits.

Second, brand attitude refers to a positive or negative evaluative response to a brand (Petty and Cacioppo 1986). If a brand provides functional, emotional, and social brand benefits to consumers, they form a positive attitude toward that brand (Keller 1993). Since a brand with a high cult status offers such benefits to consumers, we expect that consumers have a positive attitude toward a brand with a high cult status.

Third, positive word of mouth is conceptualized as the degree to which a consumer speaks well of the brand and does so in an active manner (see also Arnett, German, and Hunt 2003 who refer to promoting). It has been argued that cult followers become evangelists, spread their stories, and hire and convince others for the brand through positive word of mouth (Atkin 2004; Brady et al. 2004). Considering further that consumers often provide recommendations to individuals in their social environment, consumers are more likely to endorse a brand they trust (i.e., a brand high in persuasiveness; see Gremler, Gwinner, and Brown 2001), reducing the risk of providing wrong recommendations (Mazzarol, Sweeney, and Soutar 2007).

Prior research also shows that the love consumers feel toward a brand (Carroll and Ahuvia 2006) stimulates positive word-of-mouth communication. Brands high in cult status provide functional, emotional, and social benefits to consumers and should thus stimulate positive word of mouth. We therefore hypothesize the following:

H2a: **A brand's cult status has a positive effect on consumers' willingness to pay a price premium.**

H2b: **A brand's cult status has a positive effect on consumers' brand attitude.**

H2c: **A brand's cult status has a positive effect on consumers' positive word of mouth.**

4.7.3 Moderating Effects

The positive effects of cult brand status on consumer responses hypothesized in H2 are likely to be stronger for consumers with certain characteristics or predispositions. We therefore exemplarily explore the role of three moderating variables in the relationship between cult brand status and willingness to pay a price premium. The first likely moderator of the relationship between cult brand status and willingness to pay a price premium is public self-consciousness. Fenigstein, Scheier, and Buss (1975) conceptualized public self-consciousness as the awareness that others are aware of the self (i.e., the self as a social object). Researchers have used this concept in a consumer behavior context to asses an individual's awareness of his or her self-image and self-appearance in public (e.g., Gould and Barak 1988). People with a high public self-consciousness think more about the impression they make on others and as a consequence, focus more on how they present themselves to others (Carver and Scheier 1987; Fenigstein 1987). Therefore, in a branding context, they are more aware that others judge and rate them based on what brands they use (Malär et al. 2011). Research supports this argument by showing that publicly self-conscious individuals prefer national brands to bargain brands (Bushman 1993). We therefore hypothesize that consumers with high public self-consciousness are willing to pay a higher price for brands with a high cult status because such brands serve as an important means of self-expression.

H3a: **Public self-consciousness strengthens the relationship between a brand's cult status and consumers' willingness to pay a price premium.**

The second hypothesized moderator of the cult brand status willingness to pay a price premium relationship is self-brand connection. Self-brand connections capture the extent to which individuals incorporate a specific brand into their self-concept (Escalas and Bettman 2003). Because research shows that a set of brand associations is more meaningful the more closely the brand is linked to the consumer's self (Escalas and Bettman 2003), we expect that the relevance of the cult brand status dimensions (i.e., cultural-change orientation, following, pioneer, richness of story, persuasiveness, and distinctiveness) is higher if consumers have incorporated the underlying brand into their self-concept. That is, consumers should be willing to pay a higher price for brands with high cult status, if they have a high self-brand connection.

H3b: **Self-brand connection strengthens the relationship between a brand's cult status and consumers' willingness to pay a price premium.**

The third hypothesized moderator of the relationship between cult brand status and willingness to pay a price premium is brand involvement. Brand involvement captures consumers' interest in and personal relevance of a specific brand (Voss, Spangenberg, and Grohmann 2003). Highly involved consumers attach great value to brand use outcomes (Bloch and Richins 1983). Thus, the cult brand dimensions and their corresponding functional, emotional, and social value increase in relevance among highly involved consumers, for which they will be willing to pay a higher price. Low-involved consumers may not be willing to process a cult brand's information (e.g., cultural-change orientation) deeply. This implies that the brand is not important enough for them.

Consequently, these consumers are less likely to pay a higher price for this brand. This leads to the following hypothesis:

H3c: **Brand involvement strengthens the relationship between a brand's cult status and consumers' willingness to pay a price premium.**

4.7.4 Sample, Procedure, and Measures

A sample of 3,046 consumers (47.8% female, Median age = 24 years) participated in this study and completed the questions about one randomly assigned brand. Antecedents of cult brand status consisted of the affective and intellectual dimensions of brand experience (α = .68 and .77, respectively; Brakus, Schmitt, and Zarantonello 2009) and the hedonic nature of a brand (α = .89; Voss, Spangenberg, and Grohmann 2003). Dependent variables included willingness to pay a price premium (α = .87; Netemeyer et al. 2004), brand attitude (α = .90; Putrevu and Lord 1994), and positive word of mouth (α = .92; Arnett, German, and Hunt 2003). Public self-consciousness (α = .81; Fenigstein, Scheier, and Buss 1975), self-brand connection (α = .95; Escalas and Bettman 2005), and brand involvement (α = .82; Voss, Spangenberg, and Grohmann 2003; Zaichkowsky 1990) served as moderating variables. The criterion of Fornell and Larcker (1981) served as a basis to assess the discriminant validity of the construct measures. Discriminant validity for all constructs was supported in that the average variance extracted exceeded the squared correlations between all pairs of constructs.

4.7.5 Results

We employed AMOS 20 to model the structural relationships showed in our conceptual framework (see Figure 7). The measures of overall fit mostly met conventional standards, which suggests that our model fits the data acceptably well ($\chi^2/df = 13.21$; *NFI* = .88, *NNFI* = .88, *CFI* = .89, *SRMR* = .07, *RMSEA* = .06). Table 4 shows the results of hypotheses tests. All path coefficients in the model are significant ($p < .05$). The results support a positive relationship between the affective ($\gamma = .27$, $p \leq .01$) and intellectual ($\gamma = .11$, $p \leq .01$) dimensions of brand experience and cult brand status, as well as a positive relationship between the hedonic nature of the brand and the cult brand status ($\gamma = .57$, $p \leq .01$). Thus, H1a and H1b are supported. Further, as predicted, cult brand status has a strong positive effect on consumers' willingness to pay a price premium ($\gamma = .63$, $p \leq .01$), brand attitude ($\gamma = .68$, $p \leq .01$), and positive word of mouth ($\gamma = .69$, $p \leq .01$), supporting H2a - H2c.

THE CULT BRAND STATUS SCALE

	Standardized Regression Weights		Chi-square Differences
Antecedents of CBS			
Affective Brand Experience	.27**		
Intellectual Brand Experience	.11**		
Hedonic Nature of Brand	.57**		
Consequences of CBS			
Willingness to Pay	.63**		
Brand Attitude	.68**		
Positive Word of Mouth	.69**		
Moderating Effects of the Relationship between CBS and Willingness to Pay	**Low Cult Status**	**High Cult Status**	
Public Self-Consciousness	.55**	.69**	5.2*
Self-Brand Connection	.40**	.55**	11.2**
Brand Involvement	.37**	.56**	20.8**

$*p \leq .05$; $**p \leq .01$

Table 4: Nomological Validity Tests of the CBSS

Results also indicate a positive moderating effect of public self-consciousness, self-brand connection, and brand involvement on the relationship between cult brand status and willingness to pay a price premium. Although a brand's cult status has a positive effect on willingness to pay a price premium among consumers with a low public self-consciousness (γ = .55; p ≤ .01), low self-brand connection (γ = .40; p ≤ .01), and low brand involvement (γ = .37; p ≤ .01), the effect becomes even stronger among consumers with a high level of public self-consciousness (γ = .69; p ≤ .01), self-brand connection (γ = .55; p ≤ .01), and brand involvement (γ = .56; p ≤ .01). Chi-square difference tests (Δdf = 1) to statistically test the significance of these moderating effects supported H3a - H3c ($\Delta\chi^2$ self-consciousness = 5.2; $\Delta\chi^2$ self-brand connection = 11.2; $\Delta\chi^2$ brand involvement = 20.8; all p's < .05).

4.7.6 Discussion

From a theoretical perspective, this study relates the cult status of brands to other constructs used in the branding literature. Results suggest that the affective and intellectual dimensions of brand experience as well as the hedonic nature of brands positively relate to a brand's cult status. Cult brand status in turn positively influences relevant brand-related consumer responses (i.e., willingness to pay a price premium, brand attitude, and positive word of mouth). The effect of cult brand status on willingness to pay a price premium was significantly stronger for consumers high in public self-consciousness, self-brand connection, and brand involvement. These findings support predictions derived from theory and demonstrate the usefulness of the cult status construct in predicting important brand outcomes.

5   Conclusions and Implications

This research aimed at advancing the concept of cult brands by developing and validating a scale that measures the cult brand status—cult brand status scale (CBSS). The CBSS provides a measurement tool for the diagnosis of cult brand status than can be used by both academics and managers.

Based on an interdisciplinary conceptualization and several qualitative studies, we identified six dimensions of cult brand status: cultural-change orientation, following, pioneer, richness of story, persuasiveness, and distinctiveness. A multiphase scale development process resulted in a 24-item CBSS to measure these six dimensions. This scale is psychometrically sound and is discriminant with regard to related constructs at the overall construct level as well as at the dimensional level. Furthermore, we linked the cult brand status to theoretically and managerially relevant antecedents and outcome variables. We were able to show that the affective and intellectual aspects of brand experience as well as the hedonic nature of the brand increase a brand's cult status. A brand's cult status in turn positively influences consumer's word of mouth, brand attitude, and willingness to pay. The relationship between cult brand status and willingness to pay is even stronger for consumers high in public self-consciousness, self-brand connection, and brand involvement.

Our research advances the prior literature in conceptualizing and operationalizing a brand's cult status from a consumer perspective. First, while the phenomenon of cult brand status has been widely observed in business practice, the literature lacks a theoretically based and empirically validated explanation of what cult brand status really is: which facets does it comprise and which consumer responses does it evoke? Our research articulates the dimensions of cult brand status and delineates it from related constructs in the marketing literature, thus enhancing the understanding of the cult brand phenomenon. By providing a scale to assess a brand's cult status, researchers can use an empirically validated measurement approach for future studies that aim at contributing to our knowledge of cult brands and their marketing relevance.

Second, we offer an integrative perspective on cult status in a branding context, which is multifaceted and incorporates the complementary aspects of cultural and societal environment, brand, and consumers. Such a conceptualization extends prior views on constructs that relate to cult brand status (e.g., brand community, iconicity) by taking a broader conceptual approach and by recognizing that various factors work together and need to be considered in order to achieve cult brand status. The complex and broad nature of cult brand status may theoretically explain why it is so challenging to create cult brand status. However, it also suggests that once cult brand status is established, its complex nature protects the brand from one-dimensional imitation attempts by competitors.

Third, the cult status construct provides a possible explanation for why consumers volunteer to act as brand evangelists by strongly promoting the brand to others based on an inner conviction (Matzler, Pichler, and Hemetsberger 2007). As we were able to show a positive relationship between cult brand status and positive word-of-mouth behavior, we would expect that evangelist activities should be more common for brands high in cult status. Hence, future research could address the role of a brand's cult status in inspiring brand evangelism.

While we investigated the cult status of brands in a Western context, future research could benefit from an examination of the effect of cult brand status on consumer responses in a collectivist cultural context. It is possible that in such a context, the importance of individual dimensions of the CBSS differs (e.g., the devotion of followers with its underlying sense of belonging may be even more prominent in a collectivist cultural context) and that the strength of consumer responses to cult brand status varies.

In our nomological framework, we focused on a limited number of relevant antecedents of cult brand status, although a variety of other factors are likely to play a role. A promising avenue for future research is an investigation of other contributing factors, such as communication strategy, product design, and characteristics of a brand leader.

Further, we developed a scale to measure the current cult status of a brand. Future research could use our scale to examine the dynamics of cult brands over time. As culture is constantly evolving, a cult brand needs to respond to important cultural and societal changes in order to continuously meet new needs arising from the cultural environment. Thus, a key future research question here is how a brand can maintain its high cult status also in later stages of its life cycle.

This research has also important implications for managerial practice. We provide managers with an easy-to-administer diagnostic measurement tool to assess and track the cult status of their own and competitors' brands. Using our multidimensional CBSS, they can recognize deficient dimensions and derive strategies to strengthen these dimensions in order to increase their brand's cult status.

Furthermore, our research suggests that the creation of affective and intellectual brand experience is a critical determinant of a brand's level of cult status. Thus, managers are advised to put an emphasis on these brand experiences in order to create a high cult status for their brand. Another important insight that arose from our results is that building cult status pays off in terms of cognitive and behavioral consumer responses. Of interest to targeting and segmentation efforts is the finding that the level of a brand's cult status had a particularly pronounced effect on the willingness to pay a price premium among consumers who were already strongly involved with the brand, felt a high level of self-brand connection, and relied on brands to manage impressions (i.e., high public self-consciousness). In the management of brands that have achieved high levels of cult status, these consumers deserve particular consideration.

References

Aaker, Jennifer L. (1997), Dimensions of Brand Personality, *Journal of Marketing Research*, 34 (July), 347–356.

Aaker, Jennifer L. (1999), The Malleable Self: The Role of Self-Expression in Persuasion, *Journal of Marketing Research*, 36 (1), 45–57.

Acosta, Paul M. and Raj Devasagayam (2010), Brand Cult: Extending the Notion of Brand Communities, *Marketing Management Journal*, 20 (Spring), 165–176.

Anderson, James C. and David W. Gerbing (1993), Monte Carlo Evaluations of Goodness-of-Fit Indices for Structural Equation Models, in *Testing Structural Equation Models*, Kenneth A. Bollen and J. Scott Long, eds., Newbury Park, California: Sage Publications, Inc., 40–65.

Arnett, Dennis B., Steve H. German, and Shelby D. Hunt (2003), The Identity Salience Model of Relationship Marketing Success: The Case of Non-profit Marketing, *Journal of Marketing,* 67 (April), 89–105.

Atkin, Douglas (2004), The Culting of Brands: When Customer Become True Believers. New York: Portfolio.

Bainbridge, William S. and Rodney Stark (1979), Cult Formation: Three Compatible Models, *Sociological Analysis*, 40 (4), 283–295.

Batra, Rajeev, Aaron Ahuvia, and Richard P. Bagozzi (2011), Brand Love, *Journal of Marketing,* 76 (March), 1–16.

Belk, Russel W. and Gülnur Tumbat (2005), The Cult of Macintosh, *Consumption, Markets and Culture*, 8 (3), 205–217.

Belk, Russel W., Melanie Wallendorf, and John F. Sherry, Jr. (1989), The Sacred and the Profane in Consumer Behavior: Theodicy on the Odyssey, *Journal of Consumer Research*, 16 (1), 1–38.

Beverland, Michael (2009), *Building Brand Authenticity: 7 Habits of Iconic Brands*, New York: Palgrave Macmillan.

Bloch, Peter H. and Marsha L. Richins (1983), A Theoretical Model for the Study of Product Importance Perceptions, *Journal of Marketing*, 47 (Summer), 69–81.

Brady, Diane, Robert D. Hof, Andy Reinhardt, Moon Ihlwan, Stanley Holmes, and Kerry Capell (2004), Cult Brands, *Business Week*, August (3894), 64–67.

Brakus, Joško J., Bernd H. Schmitt, and Lia Zarantonello (2009), Brand Experience: What is it? How is it Measured? Does it Affect Loyalty?, *Journal of Marketing*, 73 (May), 52–68.

Bushman, Brad J. (1993), What's in a Name? The Moderating Role of Public Self-Consciousness on the Relation Between Brand Label and Brand Preference, *Journal of Applied Psychology*, 78 (5), 857–861.

Campbell, Colin (1977), Clarifying the Cult, *British Journal of Sociology,* 28 (3), 375–388.

Campbell, Bruce (1978), A Typology of Cults, *Sociological Analysis*, 39 (3), 228–240.

Cantril, Hadley and Muzafer Sherif (1969), The Kingdom of Father Divine, *The Journal of Abnormal and Social Psychology,* 33 (2), 174–167.

Carr, Steven D. (1996), The Cult of Brand Personality, *Marketing News*, 30 (10), 4-9.

Carroll, Barbara A. and Aaron C. Ahuvia (2006), Some Antecedents and Outcomes of Brand Love, *Marketing Letters*, 17 (2), 79–89.

Carver, Charles S. and Michael F. Scheier (1987), The Blind Men and the Elephant: Selective Examination of the Public-Private Literature Gives Rise to a Faulty Perception, *Journal of Personality*, 55 (3), 525–541.

Chalfant, Paul H., Robert E. Beckley, and Eddie C. Palmer (1986), *Religion in Contemporary Society*, Palo Alto: Mayfield.

Chitturi, Ravindra, Rajagopal Raghunathan, and Vijay Mahajan (2007), Form Versus Function: How the Intensities of Specific Emotions Evoked in Functional Versus Hedonic Trade-Offs Mediate Product Preferences, *Journal of Marketing Research*, 44 (November), 702–714.

Chitturi, Ravindra, Rajagopal Raghunathan, and Vijay Mahajan (2008), De-light by Design: The Role of Hedonic Versus Utilitarian Benefits, *Journal of Marketing*, 72 (May), 48–63.

Churchill, Gilbert A., Jr. (1979), A Paradigm for Developing Better Measures of Marketing Constructs, *Journal of Marketing Research*, 16 (February), 64–73.

Dawson, Lorne L. (2006), Comprehending Cults, the Sociology of New Religious Movements, Oxford: Oxford University Press.

Dean, Sarah (2011, September 17), Cult Film Classics "The Big Lebowski" Re-Released, Cast Reunite in New York, *The Huffington Post,* retrieved on June 5, 2012, from http://www.huffingtonpost.co.uk/2011/08/17/cult-film-classic-the-big_n_928980.html].

Douglas, Mary and Baron Isherwood (1979), *The World of Goods.* New York: Basic Books.

Ellwood, Robert (1986), The Several Meanings of Cult, *Thought,* 61 (241), 212–224.

Escalas, Jennifer E. and James R. Bettman (2003), You Are What They Eat: The Influence of Reference Groups on Consumers' Connections to Brands, *Journal of Consumer Psychology*, 13 (3), 339–348.

Escalas, Jennifer E. and James R. Bettman (2005), Self-Construal, Reference Groups, and Brand Meaning, *Journal of Consumer Research,* 32 (3), 378–389.

Fenigstein, Allan (1987), On the Nature of Public and Private Self-Consciousness, *Journal of Personality*, 55 (3), 543–554.

Fenigstein, Allan, Michael F. Scheier, and Arnold H. Buss (1975), Public and Private Self-Consciousness: Assessment and Theory, *Journal of Consulting and Clinical Psychology*, 43 (4), 522–527.

Fischer, Marc, Franziska Völckner, and Henrik Sattler (2010), How Important Are Brands? A Cross-Category, Cross-Country Study, *Journal of Marketing Research,* 47 (October), 823–839.

Fornell, Claes and David F. Larcker (1981), Evaluating Structural Equations Models with Unobservable Variables and Measurement Error, *Journal of Marketing Research*, 18 (February), 39–50.

Fournier, Susan (1994), A Consumer-Brand Relationship Framework for Strategic Brand Management, *PhD Dissertation,* University of Florida.

Glock, Charles Y. (1964), The Role of Deprivation in the Origin and Evolution of Religious Groups, in *Religion and Social Conflict,* Robert Lee and Martin E. Marty, eds., New York: Oxford University Press, 429–456.

Glock, Charles Y. and Rodney Stark (1965), *Religion and Society in Tension,* Chicago: Rand McNally.

Gori, Graham (2001, September 5), Strike at VW in Mexico Ends Unusually, *The New York Times,* retrieved on Mai 15, 2013, from http://www.nytimes.com/2001/09/06/business/strike-at-vw-in-mexico-ends-unusually.html.

Gould, Stephen J. and Benny Barak (1988), Public Self-Consciousness and Consumption Behavior, *Journal of Social Psychology*, 128 (3), 393–400.

Graeme, Douglas (2007), *I Believe in a Brand New Religion*, Haymarket Business Publications, 18–23.

Gremler, Dwayne D., Kevin P. Gwinner, and Stephen W. Brown (2001), Generating Positive Word-of-Mouth Communication Through Customer-Employee Relationships, *International Journal of Service Industry Management*, 12 (1), 44–59.

Hirschman, Elizabeth C. and Gough B. Holbrook (1982), Hedonic Consumption: Emerging Concepts, Methods and Propositions, *Journal of Marketing*, 46 (Summer), 92–101.

Holson, Laura M. (2005, May 1), Is There Life After 'Star Wars' for Lucasfilm?, *The New York Times,* retrieved on June 25, 2012, from http://query.nytimes.com/gst/fullpage.html?res=9F0DE4D71131F932A 35756C0A9639C8B63.

Holt, Douglas B. (2004), How Brands Become Icons: The Principles of Cultural Branding, Harvard Business Press.

Holt, Douglas B. and Douglas Cameron (2010), *Cultural Strategy: Using Innovative Ideologies to Build Breakthrough Brands,* Oxford: Oxford University Press.

Homburg, Christian and A. Dobratz (1992), Covariance Structure Analysis via Specification Searches, *Statistical Papers*, 33 (1), 119–142.

Homburg, Christian, Nicole Koschate, and Wayne D. Hoyer (2005), Do Satisfied Customers Really Pay More? A Study of the Relationship Between Customer Satisfaction and Willingness to Pay, *Journal of Marketing*, 69 (April), 84–96.

Hyken, Shep (2009), The Cult of the Customer: Create an Amazing Customer Experience That Turns Satisfied Customers into Customer Evangelists, New Jersey: John Wiley & Sons.

Interbrand (2011), 2011 Ranking of The Top 100 Brands, *Interbrand Website*, retrieved on September 12, 2011, from http://www.interbrand.com/en/best-global-brands/best-global-brands-2008/best-global-brands-2011.aspx.

Keiser, Thomas W. and Jacqueline L. Keiser (1987), *The Anatomy of Illusion: Religious Cults and Destructive Persuasion*, Springfield: Charles C. Thomas.

Keller, Kevin L. (1993), Conceptualizing, Measuring, and Managing Customer-Based Brand Equity, *Journal of Marketing*, 57 (January), 1–22.

Keller, Kevin L. (2001), Building Customer-Based Brand Equity: A Blueprint for Creating Strong Brands, *Marketing Science Institute*, Report Summary, 01-107, 1–31.

Kinkade, Patrick T. and Michael A. Katovich (1992), Toward a Sociology of Cult Films: Reading Rocky Horror, *Sociological Quarterly*, 33 (Summer), 191–209.

Langone, Michael D. (1993), Recovery From Cults: Help for Victims of Psychological and Spiritual Abuse, New York: W.W. Norten.

Lindstrom, Martin (2011, September 30), You Love Your iPhone—Literally, *The New York Times*, retrieved on September 24, 2012, from http://www.nytimes.com/2011/10/01/opinion/you-love-your-iphone-literally.html?_r=0.

Lofland, John (1966), *Doomsday Cult,* Englewood Cliffs, New Jersey: Prentice-Hall.

Matzler, Kurt, Elisabeth A. Pichler, and Andrea Hemetsberger (2007), Who is Spreading the Word? The Influence of Extraversion and Openness on Consumer Passion and Evangelism, *American Marketing Association's Winter Educators' Conference*, 18, 25–32.

Mazzarol, Tim, Jillian C. Sweeney, and Geoffrey, N. Soutar (2007), Conceptualizing Word-of-Mouth Activity, Triggers, and Conditions: An Exploratory Study, *European Journal of Marketing*, 41 (11/12), 1475–1494.

McAlexander, James H., John W. Schouten, and Harold F. Koenig (2002), Building Brand Community, *Journal of Marketing*, 66 (January), 38–54.

Melton, J. Gordon and Robert L. Moore (1982), *The Cult Experience: Responding to the New Religious Pluralism,* New York: Pilgrim.

Muñiz, Albert M., Jr. and Hope J. Schau (2005), Religiosity in the Abandoned Apple Newton Brand Community, *Journal of Consumer Research*, 31 (4), 737–747.

Narver, John C. and Stanley F. Slater (1999), The Effect of a Market Orientation on Business Profitability, *Journal of Marketing,* 54 (October), 20–35.

Nelson, Geoffrey K. (1969), The Spiritualist Movement and the Need for a Redefinition of Cult, *Journal of the Scientific Study of Religion,* 8 (1), 152–160.

Netemeyer, Richard G., Balaji Krishnan, Chris Pullig, Guangping Wang, Mehmet Yagci, Dwane Dean, Joe Ricks, and Ferdinand Wirth (2004), Developing and Validating Measures of Facets of Customer-Based Brand Equity, *Journal of Business Research*, 57 (2), 209–224.

Nunziata, Nick (2004, May 25), The Personality of Cult, *CNN (Cable News Network)*, retrieved on January 27, 2012 from http://edition.cnn.com/2004/SHOWBIZ/Movies/05/25/cult.films/index. html?iref=allsearch.

O'Dea, Thomas F. (1968), Sects and Cults, in *International Encyclopedia of the Social Sciences*, David L. Sills David, ed., New York, 130–136.

Okada, Erica M. (2005), Justification Effects on Consumer Choice of Hedonic and Utilitarian Goods, *Journal of Marketing Research*, 42 (February), 43–53.

Palmer, Jeff (2000), Powder Coating Provides Maximum Flexibility for Harley-Davidson, *Paint & Coatings Industry*, 16 (9), 90–92.

Park, C. Whan, Deborah J. MacInnis, Joseph Priester, Andreas B. Eisingerich, and Dawn Iacobucci (2010), Brand Attachment and Brand Attitude Strength: Conceptual and Empirical Differentiation of Two Critical Brand Equity Drivers, *Journal of Marketing*, 74 (November), 1–17.

Park, Chan S. and Vivek Srinivasan (1994), A Survey-Based Method for Measuring and Understanding Brand Equity and Its Extendibility, *Journal of Marketing Research*, 21 (May), 271–288

Perloff, Richard M. (2010), *The Dynamics of Persuasion: Communication and Attitudes in the 21st Century*, 4th Edition, New York: Lawrence Erlbaum Associates.

Petty, Richard E. and John T. Cacioppo (1986), The Elaboration Likelihood Model of Persuasion, *Advances in Experimental Social Psychology*, 19, 123–205.

Petty, Richard E. and Duane T. Wegener (1998), Attitude Change: Multiple Roles for Persuasion Variables, in *The Handbook of Social Psychology*, Daniel T. Gilbert, Susan T. Fiske, and Gardner Lindzey, eds., McGraw-Hill: New York, 323–390.

Pfautz, Harold W. (1955), The Sociology of Secularization: Religious Groups, *American Journal of Sociology*, 21 (2), 121–128.

Pham, Michel T. (2004), The Logic of Feeling, *Journal of Consumer Psychology*, 14 (4), 360–369.

Putrevu, Sanjay and Kenneth R. Lord (1994), Comparative and Non-comparative Advertising: Attitudinal Effects under Cognitive and Affective Involvement Conditions, *Journal of Advertising*, 23 (2), 77–91.

Ragas, Mattew W. and Bolivar J. Bueno (2002), The Power of Cult Branding: How 9 Magnetic Brands Turned Customers into Loyal Follower, Crown Business: New York.

Richardson, James (1978), An Oppositional and General Conceptualization of Cult, *Annual Review of the Social Science of Religion*, 2, 29–52.

Richardson, James (1979), From Cult to Sect: Creative Eclecticism in New Religious Movements, *Pacific Sociological Review*, 22 (2), 139–166.

Richardson, James (1993), Definitions of Cult: From Sociological-Technical to Popular-Negative, *Review of Religious Research*, 34 (4), 348–356.

Schouten, John W. and James H. McAlexander (1995), Subcultures of Consumption: An Ethnography of New Bikers, *Journal of Consumer Research*, 22 (1), 43–61.

Singer, Margaret T. and Janja Lalich (1995), *Cults in Our Mindset*: The Hidden Menace in Our Everyday Lives, San Francisco: Jossey-Bass.

Stark, Rodney and William S. Bainbridge (1985), *The Future of Religion: Secularization, Revival, and Cult Formation*, Berkeley, CA: University of California Press.

Swallow, D. A. (1982), Ashes and Powers: Myth, Rite and Miracle in an Indian God-Man's Cult, *Modern Asian Studies*, 16 (1), 123–158.

Voss, Kevin E., Eric R. Spangenberg, and Bianca Grohmann (2003), Measuring the Hedonic and Utilitarian Dimensions of Consumer Attitude, *Journal of Marketing Research*, 40 (August), 310–320.

Wakefield, Krik L. and James H. Barnes (1996), Retailing Hedonic Consumption: A Model of Sales Promotion of a Leisure Service, *Journal of Retailing*, 72 (4), 409–427.

Wells, Melanie (2001), Cult Brands, *Forbes*, 167 (9), 198–205.

West, Louis J. (1989), Persuasive Techniques in Contemporary Cults: A Public Health Approach, in *Cults and New Religious Movements,* Marc Galanter, ed. Washington, DC: American Psychiatric Association, 165–192.

Whitsett, Doni P. (1992), A Self Psychological Approach to the Cult Phenomenon, *Clinical Social Work Journal*, 20 (Winter), 363–375.

Woody, William D. (2009), Use of Cult in the Teaching of Psychology of Religion and Spirituality, *Psychology of Religion and Spirituality*, 1 (4), 218–232.

Yinger, J. Milton (1970), *The Scientific Study of Religion,* New York: Macmillan.

Yoo, Boonghee and Naveen Donthu (2001), Developing and Validating a Multidimensional Consumer-Based Brand Equity Scale, *Journal of Business Research,* 52 (1), 1–14.

Yoo, Boonghee, Naveen Donthu, and Sungho Lee (2000), An Examination of Selected Marketing Mix Elements and Brand Equity, *Journal of the Academy of Marketing Science*, 28 (2), 195–211.

Zaichkowsky, Judith L. (1990), The Personal Involvement Inventory: Reduction, Revision, and Application to Advertising, *Journal of Advertising*, 23 (4), 59–70.

Zarantonello, Lia and Bernd H. Schmitt (2010), Using the Brand Experience Scale to Profile Consumers and Predict Consumer Behaviour, *Journal of Brand Management*, 17 (7), 532–540.

Appendix

Factors and Items	Study 3						Study 4a						Study 4b					
	Factor Loadings	Item-to-Total Correlation	Indicator Reliabilit	Coefficient Alpha	Composite Reliability	Average Variance Extracted	Factor Loadings	Item-to-Total Correlation	Indicator Reliabilit	Coefficient Alpha	Composite Reliability	Average Variance Extracted	Factor Loadings	Item-to-Total Correlation	Indicator Reliabilit	Coefficient Alpha	Composite Reliability	Average Variance Extracted
Cultural-Change Orientation				.82	.82	.61				.85	.85	.65				.93	.91	.63
When it was first launched, "brand X" oriented itself toward changes in society.	.85	.66	.59				.88	.72	.68				.83	.82	.67			
The creation of "brand X" is based on cultural changes.	.87	.7	.65				.87	.71	.63				.75	.77	.61			
"Brand X" developed in response to new needs in society.	.87	.69	.59				.88	.72	.63				.78	.79	.66			
Following				.86	.86	.67				.82	.82	.61				.92	.9	.53
"Brand X" communicates a sense of belonging to its customers.	.87	.71	.62				.85	.67	.6				.78	.76	.62			
In a way, "brand X" has religious followers.	.89	.75	.68				.86	.67	.53				.66	.69	.54			
"Brand X" is worshipped by many consumers.	.88	.74	.71				.87	.69	.69				.75	.77	.62			
Pioneer				.91	.91	.68				.94	.94	.75				.96	.95	.75
"Brand X" is trendy.	.89	.82	.73				.93	.88	.85				.9	.88	.83			
"Brand X" is creative.	.86	.78	.67				.89	.82	.7				.88	.88	.78			
"Brand X" sets trends.	.87	.79	.72				.89	.83	.74				.91	.9	.82			
"Brand X" is "in".	.87	.78	.71				.9	.84	.8				.89	.87	.8			
"Brand X" is dynamic.	.81	.71	.55				.86	.78	.65				.87	.87	.77			

Factors and Items	Study 3						Study 4a						Study 4b					
	Factor Loadings	Item-to-Total Correlation	Indicator Reliabilit	Coefficient Alpha	Composite Reliability	Average Variance Extracted	Factor Loadings	Item-to-Total Correlation	Indicator Reliabilit	Coefficient Alpha	Composite Reliability	Average Variance Extracted	Factor Loadings	Item-to-Total Correlation	Indicator Reliabilit	Coefficient Alpha	Composite Reliability	Average Variance Extracted
Richness of Story				.76	.76	.51				.78	.79	.55				.9	.88	.64
"Brand X's" philosophy is passed on from generation to generation.	.81	.58	.55				.81	.59	.54				.8	.8	.64			
There is a special history behind "brand X".	.82	.59	.5				.84	.62	.55				.8	.81	.67			
"Brand X" has a long history.	.83	.6	.48				.86	.66	.56				.7	.77	.61			
Persuasiveness				.92	.92	.63				.94	.94	.7				.97	.97	.8
"Brand X" is a trustworthy brand.	.89	.84	.79				.9	.85	.78				.9	.92	.87			
"Brand X" is a credible brand.	.88	.82	.78				.9	.86	.79				.9	.91	.84			
"Brand X" is an honest brand.	.83	.75	.66				.85	.79	.68				.9	.89	.83			
"Brand X" is genuine.	.82	.74	.63				.86	.8	.71				.8	.87	.77			
"Brand X" provides high quality products/services.	.8	.73	.53				.84	.79	.65				.9	.89	.83			
"Brand X" has proven itself.	.76	.68	.5				.86	.8	.69				.8	.81	.67			
"Brand X" is known for superior performance or quality.	.77	.7	.49				.83	.77	.62				.88	.86	.8			
Distinctiveness				.82	.83	.62				.81	.81	.59				.89	.89	.66
Products and services offered by "brand X" are easily recognized.	.88	.7	.64				.86	.67	.58				.76	.74	.56			
"Brand X" is distinctive.	.9	.74	.75				.87	.69	.65				.8	.77	.64			
"Brand X" distinguishes itself actively from its competitors.	.79	.57	.47				.82	.61	.54				.8	.79	.65			

150

Factors and Items	Study 5						Study 6					
	Factor Loadings	Item-to-Total Correlation	Indicator Reliabilit	Coefficient Alpha	Composite Reliability	Average Variance Extracted	Factor Loadings	Item-to-Total Correlation	Indicator Reliabilit	Coefficient Alpha	Composite Reliability	Average Variance Extracted
Cultural-Change Orientation				.81	.81	.59				.84	.84	.64
When it was first launched, "brand X" oriented itself toward changes in society.	.83	.63	.53				.86	.69	.63			
The creation of "brand X" is based on cultural changes.	.85	.67	.61				.89	.74	.69			
"Brand X" developed in response to new needs in society.	.87	.69	.64				.86	.69	.61			
Following				.83	.83	.62				.8	.8	.57
"Brand X" communicates a sense of belonging to its customers.	.85	.67	.59				.81	.59	.5			
In a way, "brand X" has religious followers.	.86	.68	.54				.87	.69	.59			
"Brand X" is worshipped by many consumers.	.88	.72	.73				.85	.65	.63			
Pioneer				.94	.94	.77				.94	.94	.74
"Brand X" is trendy.	.93	.88	.86				.89	.83	.75			
"Brand X" is creative.	.88	.82	.68				.89	.82	.72			
"Brand X" sets trends.	.91	.85	.79				.91	.85	.78			
"Brand X" is "in".	.92	.82	.84				.9	.84	.78			
"Brand X" is dynamic.	.87	.8	.66				.87	.8	.69			

Factors and Items	Study 5						Study 6					
	Factor Loadings	Item-to-Total Correlation	Indicator Reliabilit	Coefficient Alpha	Composite Reliability	Average Variance Extracted	Factor Loadings	Item-to-Total Correlation	Indicator Reliabilit	Coefficient Alpha	Composite Reliability	Average Variance Extracted
Richness of Story				.75	.76	.51				.8	.81	.58
"Brand X"s" philosophy is passed on from generation to generation.	.81	.57	.52				.68	.59	.46			
There is a special history behind "brand X".	.85	.62	.59				.86	.7	.73			
"Brand X" has a long history.	.81	.57	.43				.75	.66	.56			
Persuasiveness				.91	.91	.59				.93	.93	.65
"Brand X" is a trustworthy brand.	.86	.79	.73				.86	.79	.74			
"Brand X" is a credible brand.	.88	.81	.78				.9	.85	.85			
"Brand X" is an honest brand.	.81	.73	.65				.87	.8	.78			
"Brand X" is genuine.	.8	.72	.58				.85	.79	.7			
"Brand X" provides high quality products/services.	.76	.68	.46				.82	.75	.52			
"Brand X" has proven itself.	.74	.65	.45				.79	.73	.49			
"Brand X" is known for superior performance or quality.	.76	.67	.45				.78	.71	.46			
Distinctiveness				.81	.82	.6				.84	.84	.64
Products and services offered by "brand X" are easily recognized.	.86	.66	.58				.87	.7	.63			
"Brand X" is distinctive.	.9	.73	.7				.9	.76	.74			
"Brand X" distinguishes itself actively from its competitors.	.8	.58	.52				.84	.65	.55			

PAPER 3

Cult Branding in a Specific Cultural Context: The Generation Me[6]

A number of researchers, especially in sociology, have claimed that in many industrialized Western societies, a new cultural change has occurred over the last years: They claim to have observed the rise of the self-focused consumer, the Generation Me (e.g., Twenge 2006; Twenge and Campbell 2009). If this observation is true, managers should ask themselves how they can attract such narcissistic consumers and how they should design their branding activities in order to do so. Since a typical consumer of Generation Me seems to have a very particular personality (i.e., highly narcissistic), he might be attracted to brands that also have a specific personality. In the context of this dissertation, it is especially interesting to know whether a self-focused consumer feels more attracted to a cult brand that is closer to his or her actual self (authentic branding strategy) or to his or her ideal self (aspirational branding strategy). We show that highly narcissistic consumers show very positive emotions toward authentic branding strategies, but no significant emotional response to an aspirational branding strategy. In contrast, less-narcissistic consumers respond positively to both branding strategies. The managerial and academic implications of these findings are discussed.

---

[6] A very different earlier version of this paper has been successfully submitted and presented at the European Marketing Academy Conference, Ljubljana, 2011. It is based on a joint work with Lucia Malär and Bettina Nyffenegger.

1   Introduction

People in the baby boomer generation grew up in the 1950s and in the early 1960s, a rather collectivistic time (Howe and Strauss 2000). Boomers were more focused on the group-oriented ethos and cared about the well-being of the group they lived in. In the 1970s, Western culture has experienced a change toward focusing on the individual and on the need of the self (Firat and Venkatesh 1993; Fukuyama 1999). People born after 1970 were more self-focused and narcissistic. In this so-called Generation Me, it is literally "all about me" and about "being yourself" (Twenge and Campbell 2009). Generation Me tends to put its own needs first and focuses on feeling good about themselves. One can easily realize this cultural shift when taking a closer look at individual-focused reality TV shows, the amount of personal blogs, and the specific use of social networking sites such as Facebook, Instagram, Pinterest, and Twitter in order to express themselves. Such social networking sites play a specific role in identity construction and self-presentation (Nadkarni and Hofmann 2011). Facebook, in particular, enables users to set up a public or semi-public profile, which consist consists of information on gender, date of birth, contact details (e.g., cell phone number, e-mail address), hometown, education, personal interests, etc. In many cases, users also share a number of pictures and videos or post status updates to inform friends about such things like feelings, opinions, activities, and whereabouts (Facebook 2013). In their study, Buffardi and Campbell (2008) examined the association between narcissism and Facebook use. Not surprisingly, their results revealed a positive relation between narcissistic personality traits and the use of Facebook—particularly profiles and photos—to express themselves. Buffardi and Campbell (2008) analyzed Facebook profiles and revealed that highly narcissistic consumers, first, spend more time on Facebook and, second, are more likely to upload pictures where they look great and fashionable. These Facebook users are obviously highly concerned about their physical appearance—a narcissistic behavior (Vazire et al. 2008). The fact that Facebook is mainly being used for two social needs: "need to belong" and "need for self-presentation" (Nadkarni and Hofmann 2011), in conjunction with the fact that Facebook is being used by more than 70% of America's teens below the age of 17 (Lenhart et al. 2010), it is apparent that narcissism is increasingly relevant. In addition, in their book *The Narcissistic Epidemic,* Twenge and Campbell (2009, p. 1) put it this way: "There are more narcissists than ever . . ."

According to conceptual considerations in psychology theory, narcissists are people who see themselves as "special, superior, and entitled and who are prone to exhibitionism and vanity" (Sedikides et al. 2007, p. 254). They also exhibit egocentrism and self-importance and think they have unlimited ability and power. More often than not, narcissistic people also tend to have a strong need for attention as well as admiration (Sedikides et al. 2007). Narcissistic characteristics can be operationalized by means of the Narcissistic Personality Inventory (NPI; Raskin and Hall 1979), which is the most popular and valid measure of narcissism. Based on the NPI, a narcissist is an individual that scores high on the NPI. The NPI consists of seven subscales, which are as follows: authority, entitlement, exhibitionism, exploitation, self-sufficiency, superiority, and vanity (Sedikides et al. 2007; Raskin and Hall 1981; Raskin and Terry 1988). Additionally, based on the NPI, several authors found evidence for a remarkable rise in narcissistic personality traits in society (e.g., Fukuyama 1999; Gough 1979; Trzesniewski et al. 2008; Twenge et al. 2008).

Against the background of an increasingly narcissistic society, we suggest that understanding today's Generation Me—and, more generally, to keeping up with such generational changes—becomes crucial for branding.

Although personality and social psychology have given considerable attention to narcissism (Morf and Rhodewalt 2001; Vazire and Funder 2006), empirical research on the impact on branding and consumer behavior of such a sociocultural change is rather scarce. Conceptually, it has been argued that narcissists are more attracted to high-prestige products and are more interested in the symbolic rather than utilitarian value of products. Generally speaking, narcissistic consumers are interested in products that cast them in the most favorable light. Narcissistic consumers are also more likely to live a more expensive lifestyle—changing cars frequently, spending on designer clothes, and joining exclusive clubs or restaurants (Sedikides et al. 2007).

Since this dissertation is focused on cult brands, in our research, we extend the conceptual framework of Malär et al. (2011) to a cult brand context in which we analyze the role of actual versus ideal self-congruence on the relationship of emotional brand attachment (EBA) among highly narcissistic consumers. We show that highly narcissistic consumers show very positive emotions toward authentic branding strategies, but no significant emotional response in the case of an aspirational branding strategy. In this research paper, we examine how such a sociocultural change—the change in the dominant personality traits of an entire generation—affects the EBA of lowly versus highly narcissistic individuals toward cult brands. We then try to derive suggestions on how to position cult brands in order to attract consumers with a more narcissistic personality. By doing so, we follow the suggestion of Malär et al. (2011) that "further research might consider other moderating effects, particularly product-related context variables."

2 Conceptualization and Hypotheses

With reference to Malär et al. (2011), the concept of *self-congruence* can serve us in investigating the relationship between the self-concept and the EBA. With reference to Aaker (1999) and Sirgy (1982), Malär et al. (2011) describe self-congruence as a concept that represents the fit between a consumer's self and the personality or image of a brand. As proposed, the concept can affect consumer responses to a brand (Aaker 1999; Grohmann 2009) and consequently also play an important role for EBA (Park et al. 2010). The article of Malär et al. (2011) shows that product involvement, self-esteem, and public self-consciousness can moderate this relation. In this paper, we extend this framework by examining the moderating role of narcissism on the relationship between the self-concept and the emotional attachment toward cult brands.

It is widely known that individuals judge others based on what they eat, wear, and drive. In other words, individuals make inferences about what consumption goods people purchase (e.g., motor vehicle) and what kind of services they consume (e.g., restaurants). This same prejudicial behavior of individuals or groups does not only have a negative connotation but can also be systematically used as a means for self-expression. Accordingly, individuals prefer products with images that are congruent with their own images (Belk, Bahn, and Mayer 1982). So products can help consumers to define themselves. This fact makes consumers purchase brands that help them express who they are or who they would like to be. Consequently, consumers buy and use brands with a specific personality to express their self-concept (Aaker 1999). Brand personality is a concept that ascribes particular human characteristics to a brand based on how a consumer perceives that particular brand (Aaker 1997). This concept can be helpful for consumers to either express their actual or ideal self (Aaker 1999).

According to prior research (Belch 1978; Belch and Landon 1977; Delozier 1972) the self-concept has two components: the actual self and the ideal self. Both forms represent an individual's self-perception. While the actual self is a more realistic perception of oneself, the ideal self consists of the imagination of ideals related to what a person would like to become (Wylie 1979). A brand's personality that fits either the consumer's actual or ideal self can lead to self-congruence. More specifically, actual self-congruence, on the one hand, reflects how the consumer perceives the fit between his or her actual self and the brand personality. Ideal self-congruence, on the other hand, means the perceived fit between the brand personality and the consumer's ideal self. In other words, an actually self-congruent brand represents who the consumer actually is, while an ideally self-congruent brand depicts who the consumer would like to be (Aaker 1999).

We propose that actual and ideal self-congruence both affect the con-sumers' EBA. According to Park et al. (2010), EBA is a good indicator of strong consumer-brand relationships. The relationship between consumers and brands in turn are reliable sources of future revenues and profits. Finally, we propose that narcissism moderates the relationship between actual self-congruence or ideal self-congruence and EBA. As we have learned earlier, narcissists see themselves as more special, superior, and entitled than others do (Campbell, Rudich, and Sedikides 2002; Raskin and Hall 1981; Raskin and Terry 1988). Furthermore, they are prone to vanity and exhibitionism, want to earn the admiration of others by purchasing high-prestige products, and are strongly influenced by self-image motives (Ames, Rose, and Anderson 2006; Sedikides et al. 2007). Thus, we suggest that narcissism most likely has a rein-forcing impact on the relation between the type of self-congruence (i.e., actual or ideal self-congruence) and EBA. Understanding this interaction can have crucial implications for the definition of a brand personality when positioning a brand to attract narcissists.

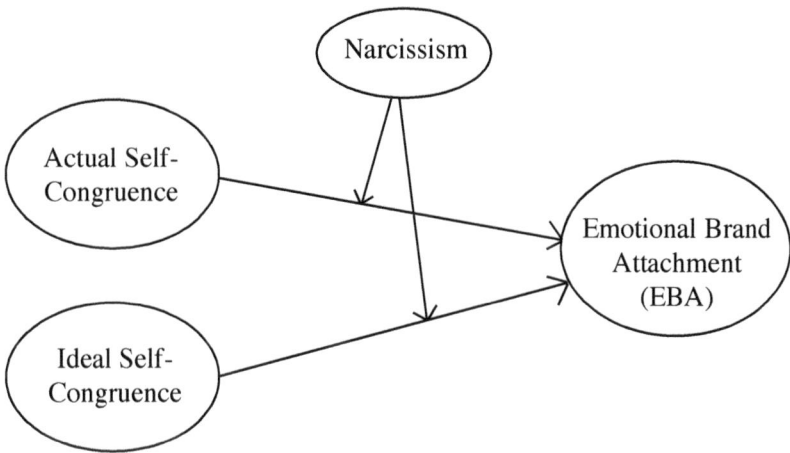

Figure 8: Framework of the Hypotheses Testing

In line with Malär et al. (2011), the first two hypotheses of this paper refer to the impact of actual and ideal self-congruence on EBA and thereby lay down the background for hypotheses 3 and 4, where we have a closer look at how narcissistic personality traits affect this relationship.

2.1   Hypotheses 1 and 2: The Effect of ASC and ISC on EBA

The first hypothesis refers to the relationship between actual self-congruence on EBA toward cult brands. In this case, the self-verification theory (Swann 1983) plays a central role. This theory proposes that individuals prefer to be seen by others as they see themselves. If a person sees himself or herself as nice, he wants to be perceived as nice by others. In sum, the self-verification theory depicts that people seek self-confirming reactions from others. In other words, according to the self-verification theory, individuals strive for confirmation of their existing self-concepts. This means that people do not want to change their self-concepts to match a specific behavior; rather, they want to confirm and reinforce their existing self-concepts (Swann and Read 1980). Whether an individual's self-view is positive or negative, according to the self-verification theory, people behave according to how they see themselves (Lecky 1945). In other words, people use their social interactions to gather feedback that verifies their self-concepts (Swann and Read 1980).

In the context of cult branding, consumers can validate their self-concept by purchasing and using a brand whose personality is congruent with his or her actual self. Such consumption leads to a positive reinforcement of the consumer, which, in turn, can increase the EBA toward this cult brand. Based on this argument and according to Malär et al. (2011), we hypothesize:

H1:   **Actual self-congruence has a positive effect on the EBA towards cult brands.**

While we have argued that the self-verification theory relates to actual self-congruence, we now introduce the idea of the self-enhancement theory in conjunction with ideal self-congruence. The theory of self-enhancement proposes that people are striving to increase their perception of personal worth and value (Sedikides and Strube 1997). Some authors even argue that self-enhancement is a crucial goal of mankind (Allport 1937). In other words, striving for more must be every individual's goal. So self-enhancement theorists suggest that all people aim to improve other people's perception of themselves. That is to say, they want others to think well of them. Putting this theory in a branding context means that an ideally self-congruent brand, which is a brand whose personality reflects the consumer's ideal self, can support the consumer getting closer to his or her ideal self (Grubb and Grathwohl 1967).

Based on these considerations, we claim that consumers who see their dreams embodied in a brand will feel more emotionally attached to it.

H2:   **Ideal self-congruence has a positive effect on the EBA toward cult brands.**

2.2   Hypothesis 3: The Effect of Narcissism on the Relation between ASC and EBA

We propose narcissism as moderator of the relationship between self-congruence and EBA. We take the view that this personality trait impacts our base model relation—on the actual self-congruence side—for one main reason: as introduced earlier, narcissists believe that they are unique, special, and grandiose (Rhodewalt and Morf 1995). Because of the superior perception of themselves, their need and motivation for self-enhancement is rather low. They already are "in love" with their actual self and do not strive for some ideal to the same extent as less-narcissistic consumers. In our context of brand positioning, this means that highly narcissistic consumers are less likely to perceive benefits from self-enhancement resulting from an ideally self-congruent brand. They already see themselves as perfect and thus are not attracted by brands that convey ideal personalities. In other words, they will not experience positive emotions toward the brand in the case of an aspirational branding strategy (i.e., ideal self-congruence). Rather, they seek to confirm their actual excessively positive self-views and hence are more likely to feel attracted by brands that reflect their own personality, which applies more in the case of authentic brands. Based on the self-verification process, narcissistic consumers will feel closer toward a brand that reflects their actual self (Swann 1983). Based on this argumentation, we suggest that narcissistic consumers have more positive feelings towards a brand that verifies, confirms, and expresses their actual self-concept.

H3:   **Narcissism has a positive moderating effect on the relationship between actual self-congruence and the EBA toward cult brands.**

2.3   Hypothesis 4: The Effect of Narcissism on the Relation between ISC and EBA

For this hypothesis, we hypothesize the same moderator—narcissism. However, in this case, we argue that narcissism affects our base model relation mainly via the ideal self-congruence: In contradiction to highly narcissistic consumers, less-narcissistic consumers do not feel superior to others, are not entitled, and do not want to put themselves in a perfect light. Such consumers might even be aware of their imperfections. As a consequence, they are less likely to be fully satisfied with their actual self. Hence, they should be more prone toward self-enhancement via an ideally self-congruent brand (Higgins 1987; Markus and Wurf 1987). As a consequence, they are more attracted to brands that represent who they would like to be because these ideally self-congruent brands, help them improve themselves. Through the consumption of such brands, these lowly narcissistic people believe to overcome their imperfections. Based on that, such consumers will experience positive emotions resulting from a sym-bolic self-improvement. In other words, consumers with a low level of narcis-sism are more likely to see their aspirations and dreams embodied in a brand (than narcissistic consumers) and will hence emotionally connect with brands that fit their ideal self (aspirational branding strategy).

H4: **Narcissism has a negative moderating effect on the relation-ship between ideal self-congruence and EBA toward cult brands.**

3   Research and Results

In this chapter, we provide information on the research design, introduce the methodology, and present the results.

3.1   Design and Methodology

We carried out a large-scale online study with respondents from a variety of educational and professional backgrounds. In total, 512 participants (55.1% female; average age of 28) completed the online questionnaire. The question-naire started with an introductory text providing information about the proce-dure and the possibility to participate in a lottery as an incentive. Then the participants were randomly assigned to one of the 57 cult brands and had, after reporting the brand familiarity on the scale of Kent and Allen (1994),[7] to an-swer the questions for only one cult brand. The brand familiarity had to be higher than 3.5 (5 = *maximum*); otherwise, a new cult brand was randomly assigned.

We used empirically validated scales and measured them with five-point Likert-scales anchored by *strongly disagree* and *strongly agree*. For the assessment of the independent variables' actual and ideal self-congruence, we used a two-step approach according to Malär et al. 2011. In a first step, partici-pants took their time to think about the cult brand's personality and thought about their actual and ideal self.

---

[7] I feel very familiar with brand x; I feel very experienced with brand x; I know the product(s) of brand x.

In the second step, they indicated the extent of actual and ideal self-congruence with two items according to Sirgy et al. (1997):

1) The personality of brand x is consistent with either *how I see myself* (my actual self), or with how *I would like to be* (my ideal self)

2) The personality of brand x is a *mirror image of me* (my actual self) or is a mirror image of the person *I would like to be* (my ideal self).

We assessed the dependent variable—EBA—with six items previously used by Thomson, MacInnis, and Park (2005): "My feelings towards the brand can be characterized by affection, love, connection, passion, delight, and captivation." Finally, we measured the moderating variable narcissism with the widely used Narcissistic Personality Inventory (NPI-16; Ames, Rose, and Anderson 2005).

Overall, our measurement scales were reliable and valid. For instance, all coefficient alpha values exceed the threshold value of .7 recommended by Nunnally (1978): actual self-congruence .83, ideal self-congruence .95, EBA .89, and narcissism .72. Also, the degree of the discriminant validity for all our constructs is sufficient (Fornell and Larcker 1981).

3.2 Results

We employed AMOS 20 to model the relationships of our conceptual framework shown in Figure 7. The model had well fit values ($\chi2/df$ = 5.51, *RMSEA* = .09, *SRMR* = .05, *NFI* = .93, *NNFI* = .92, and *CFI* = .94). Based on our results, we can confirm a strong positive relationship between actual self-congruence and EBA (γ = .53, $p \leq .01$), supporting Hypothesis 1. In contrast, ideal self-congruence does not have a significant effect on EBA (γ = .08, n.s.). Hypothesis 2 is therefore not supported. Together, actual and ideal self-congruence explain 36 percent of the variance of EBA (see Figure 9).

Base Model

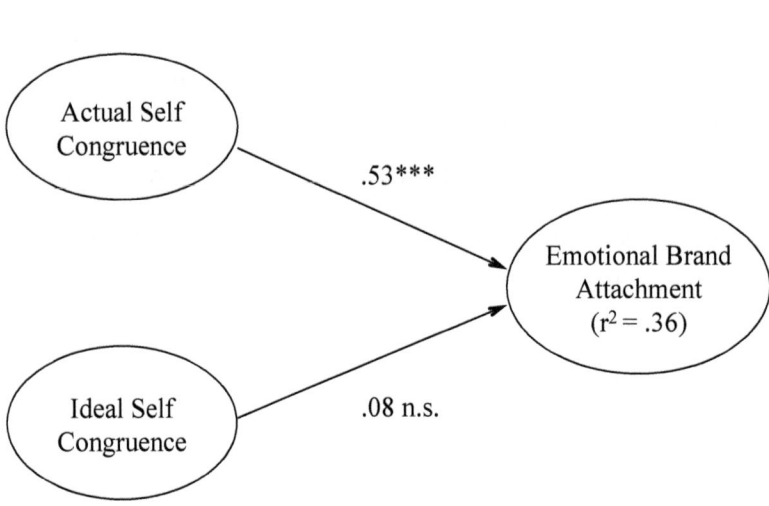

$$*p \leq .1; **p \leq .05; ***p \leq .01$$

Figure 9: Test Results for Hypotheses 1 and 2 (Base Model)

We employed multiple-group (i.e., low and high narcissism) structural equation modeling to test Hypotheses 3 and 4. The results indicate a positive moderating effect of narcissism on the examined relationship. More specifically, actual self-congruence has a stronger positive effect on EBA among high NPI-assessed consumers ($\gamma = .85$; $p \le .01$), compared with low NPI-assessed consumers ($\gamma = .37$; $p \le .01$; see Figure 10 and Figure 11). In the next step, we tested the significance of this moderating effect statistically relying on a chi-square difference test. Supporting Hypothesis 3, the chi-square difference with $\Delta d.f. = 1$ is significant at the .05-level ($\Delta\chi2_{ASC} = 4.04$).

Moderated Model: High Narcissism

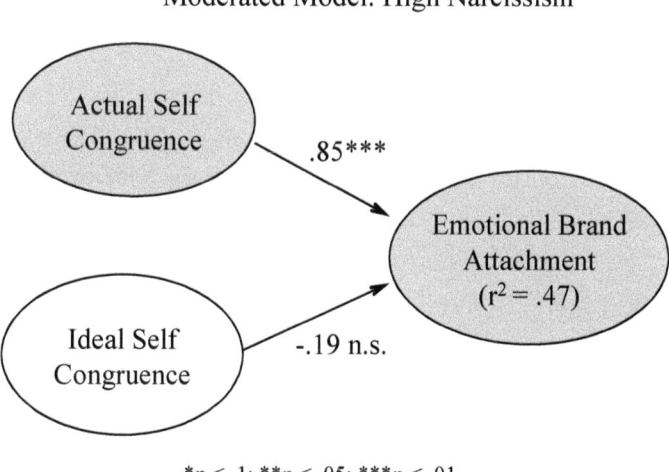

$*p \le .1; **p \le .05; ***p \le .01$

Figure 10: Test Results for Hypothesis 3 (High Narcissism)

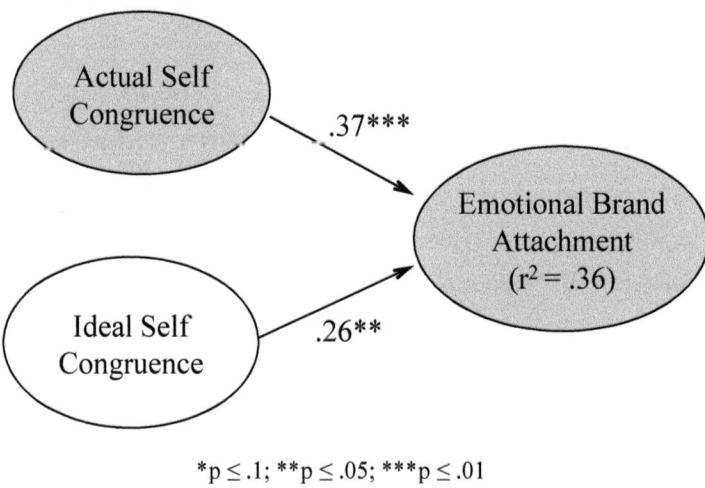

Figure 11: Test Results for Hypothesis 3 (Low Narcissism)

In contrast, ideal self-congruence has a significant and positive effect on EBA only among consumers that showed a low level of narcissism ($\gamma = .26$; $p \leq .05$). Furthermore, no significant effect among highly narcissistic consumers was found ($\gamma = -.19$; n.s.; see Figure 12 and Figure 13). The chi-square difference again is significant ($\Delta\chi^2_{ISC} = 4.27$; $\Delta d.f. = 1$; $p \leq .05$), thereby supporting Hypothesis 4 (H4).

Moderated Model: High Narcissism

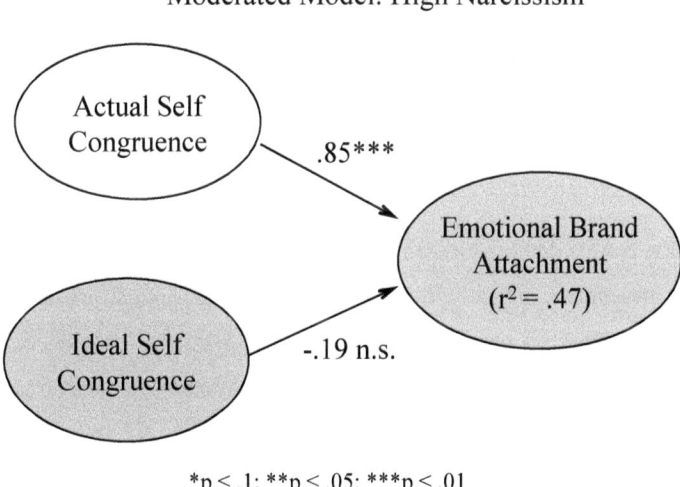

*$p \leq .1$; **$p \leq .05$; ***$p \leq .01$

Figure 12: Test Results for Hypothesis 4 (High Narcissism)

Moderated Model: Low Narcissism

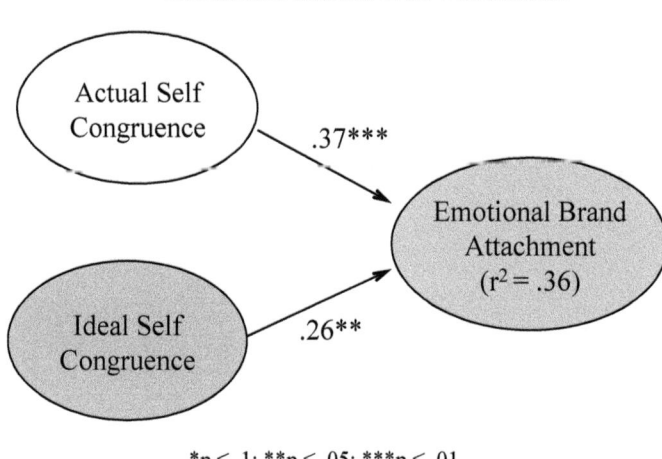

$$^*p \leq .1; ^{**}p \leq .05; ^{***}p \leq .01$$

Figure 13: Test Results for Hypothesis 4 (Low Narcissism)

In sum, the results demonstrate a remarkable moderating impact of the personality trait narcissism on the relation between actual and ideal self-congruence and EBA. In the next chapter, we interpret these results, provide future research suggestions, and present managerial implications.

4   Conclusions, Future Research, and Implications for Managers

This research paper first aimed at examining the effect of actual versus ideal self-congruence on consumers' EBA to cult brands. Second, we investigated whether the growing narcissistic personality trait of individuals in Western society affects this relationship. To that end, we measured the impact of the moderator variable narcissism on the relationship between self-congruence and EBA. Accordingly, we have proposed that the strength of the relationship between actual and ideal self-congruence and EBA in a cult brand context depends on the narcissistic personality trait of consumers.

Our findings for the basic model were in line with those of Malär et al. (2011): The basic model revealed a positive impact of actual self-congruence on EBA, whereas ideal self-congruence did not significantly affect EBA. It comes as no surprise therefore that in our specific cult brand context, consumers prefer to form a connection with a brand that reflects who they actually are than with a brand that pretends to help them achieve a specific ideal. The moderated model (i.e., low narcissism and high narcissism) showed that the effect of actual self-congruence on EBA increases among highly narcissistic consumers (see Hypothesis 3). This means that narcissists emotionally attach even stronger to actual self-congruent brands. In Hypothesis 4, we showed that narcissism has a negative effect on the relationship between ideal self-congruence and EBA. In other words, consumers scoring low in terms of narcissism emotionally attach to brands that represent their ideal self.

4.1   Academic Implications and Future Research

This research paper extends the knowledge basis of the framework of Malär et al. (2011) to the context of cult brands. Our findings revealed that among cult brands, the relation between actual self-congruence and EBA is strong. At the same time, this fact confirms the relevance of brand personality for cult brands. This applies even more since brand personality is a key facet of brand identity whose strong importance for cult brands has been noted earlier in this disserta- tion. On the side of the dependent variable, however, for cult brands, not only the emotional attachment plays an important role, but also to keep the level of attachment for a longer period of time is a pivotal objective. Since emotional attachment predicts loyalty (Thomson, McInnis, and Park 2005), an interesting research approach could be to take this model a step further. Since loyalty is captured in the main characteristics of cult brands or in a "cult following," the examination of the relation of self-congruence and loyalty toward cult brands could increase the knowledge in this matter to a large extent. We have learned earlier in this dissertation the importance of word of mouth, especially for cult brands. Therefore, another interesting research approach could be to shed light on the effects of self-congruence on word of mouth. We would assume in this matter that because of the self-verification process (Swann and Read 1980), actually self-congruent brands benefit to a higher degree of this relation than ideally self-congruent brands. With regard to pricing decisions we would ex- pect that the ideal self-concept plays a more prominent role as consumers might be willing to spend more money on brands that help to bring them closer to what they would like to be (i.e., increased willingness to pay, as for in- stance, in the luxury-brand industry). Moreover, Tian, Bearden, and Hunter (2001) argue that consumers purchase and consume products for the purpose to feel different from others. Since uniqueness plays an important role in a cult brand context, the effect of self-congruence on the consumers' need for uniqueness could provide important knowledge.

Furthermore, we consider the examination of the role of narcissism on the relation between self-congruence on EBA as an important academic contribution. Since narcissism is characterizing today's consumption-relevant generations, further research should be dedicated to the closer investigation of narcissism, not only in the presented framework, but also on a more general level. Research questions in this regard could address the examination of the self-verification process for narcissistic consumers. Since narcissists are more self-focused and egocentric, they might not be likely to act as devoted followers of a brand or participate in brand communities. Their feeling of being superior might be incompatible with showing affection or devotion toward a specific brand. Against this background, it would be interesting to analyze more closely their relationship to cult brands, particularly when it comes to showing such passion for a brand or act like followers.

4.2   Managerial Implications

Our results also have important implications for marketing managers of cult brands. On a general level, marketers are increasingly interested in finding ways to create strong brands, for instance by developing strong EBA among their consumers. Such strong EBA can induce stronger brand loyalty and also brand performance (Park et al. 2010). As noted earlier, narcissism as an individual personality trait has increased recently. In literature, it is argued that people who were born in the 1970s, 1980s, and 1990s are on average more narcissistic than any previous generation (Twenge and Campbell 2009). Basically, narcissism has broadened from being an individual personality trait to characterizing a whole generation and thereby becoming a phenomenon of sociocultural relevance. We assume that this sociocultural change has even affected how society perceives narcissism, shifting from a universally negative trait to a more accepted characteristic. Assuming that the acceptance level of narcissism in society has indeed increased, being able to anticipate such sociocultural changes is a key challenge in branding, more specifically in dealing with the question of how to position brands in a more narcissistic societal environment. Our results show how important knowing the cultural context of a brand's target group is. More specifically, our findings can provide guidance on how to position brands when trying to attract more narcissistic consumers. While our results suggest that, in a cult brand context, the actual self is more important for consumers' EBA, such an authentic branding approach becomes even more important when targeting narcissistic consumers. As our results revealed, the relationship between actual self-congruence and EBA is stronger among highly narcissistic consumers. Such consumers apparently are more likely to connect to a brand that reflects who they are. This fact can be linked to the construct of authenticity (Harter 2002), meaning that people scoring high on the NPI prefer to behave in a more genuine and less-artificial way. Particularly in a cult brand context, our results clearly point out the importance of authentic branding in a market environment, in which marketers have to deal with growing narcissistic personality traits. Cult brands, as shown earlier in this dissertation, have a clear connection to a subcultural context and hence convey authentic rather than artificial values. This fact might also be a reason for cult brand's success in the market. In sum, we can suggest, particularly for cult brands, pursuing an authentic branding strategy, as for instance, embodied in the Dove advertisement in Figure 14.

Figure 14: Dove Advertisement "Authentic Brand Positioning"
(Actual Character)[8]

However, while authentic branding applied by brands such as Dove, L'Occitane en Provence, and Whole Foods seems to become more relevant in management practice (Gilmore and Pine 2007; Beverland and Farrelly 2010), aspirational branding strategies may still work. Our results indicate that this may be the case, especially among consumers scoring low in narcissism. We assume that these people might be less self-confident, need more guidance, and are thus more likely to be attracted by brands that represent ideals as Beyoncé's Fragrance Heat Rush Advertisement in Figure 15.

---

[8] Source: www.adforum.com

Figure 15: Heat Rush "Aspirational Brand Positioning" (Ideal Character)[9]

However, against the background of a growing narcissistic society a shift toward more authentic branding strategies could pay off. Nevertheless, such cultural changes might change earlier than expected. Because of that, it is highly instrumental for cult brand managers to periodically analyze such cultural changes since they have to anticipate such changes for both the creation of new cult brands and the management of existing ones.

---

[9] Source: www.luxatic.com

References

Aaker, Jennifer L. (1997), Dimensions of Brand Personality, *Journal of Marketing Research*, 34 (3), 347–56.

Aaker, Jennifer L. (1999), The Malleable Self: The Role of Self-Expression in Persuasion, *Journal of Marketing Research*, 36 (1), 45–57.

Allport, Gordon W. (1937), *Personality: A Psychological Interpretation*, New York: Holt.

Ames, Daniel R., Paul Rose, and Cameron P. Anderson (2006), The NPI-16 as a Short Measure of Narcissism, *Journal of Research in Personality*, 40, 440–450.

Belch, George E. (1978), Belief Systems and the Differential Role of the Self-Concept, in *Advances in Consumer Research*, Keith Hunt and Ann Arbor, eds., MI: Association for Consumer Research, 320–325.

Belch, George E. and Laird Landon, Jr. (1977), Discriminant Validity of a Product-Anchored Self-Concept Measure, *Journal of Marketing Research*, 14 (May), 252–256.

Belk, Russel W., Kenneth D. Bahn, and Robert N. Mayer (1982), Development Recognition of Consumption Symbolism, *Journal of Consumer Research*, 9, 4–17.

Beverland, Michael B. and Francis J. Farrelly (2010), The Quest for Authenticity in Consumption: Consumers' Purposive Choice of Authentic Cues to Shape Experienced Outcomes, *Journal of Consumer Research*, 36 (5), 838–856.

Buffardi, Laura E. and W. Keith Campbell (2008), Narcissism and Social Networking Web Sites, *Personality and Social Psychology Bulletin*, 34 (10), 1303–1314.

Campbell, W. Keith, Erich A. Rudich, Constantine Sedikides (2002), Narcissism, Self-Esteem, and The Positivity of Self-Views: Two Portraits of Self-Love, *Personality and Social Psychology Bulletin*, 28, 358–368.

Delozier, Maynard W. and Rollie Tillman (1972), Self-Image Concepts—Can They Be Used to Design Marketing Programs? *Southern Journal of Business,* 7 (1), 9–15.

Facebook (2013), *Facebook Help Site*, retrieved on November 15, 2013, from https://www.facebook.com/help/?ref=pf.

Firat, A. Fuat and Alladi Venkatesh (1993), Postmodernity: The Age of Marketing, *International Journal of Research in Marketing,* 10 (3), 227–249.

Fornell, Claes and David F. Larcker (1981), Evaluating Structural Equation Models With Unobservable Variables and Measurement Error, *Journal of Marketing Research*, 18 (1), 39–50.

Fukuyama, Francis (1999), The Great Disruption: Human Nature and the Reconstitution of Social Order, New York: Free Press.

Gilmore, James H. and B. Joseph Pine II (2007), *Authenticity: What Consumers Really Want*, Boston: Harvard Business School Press.

Gough, Harrison G. (1979), A Creative Personality Scale for the Adjective Check List, *Journal of Personality and Social Psychology*, 37 (8), 1398–1405.

Grohmann, Bianca (2009), Gender Dimensions of Brand Personality, *Journal of Marketing Research*, 46 (1), 105–19.

Grubb, Edward L. and Harrison L. Grathwohl (1967), Consumer Self-Concept, Symbolism and Market Behavior: A Theoretical Approach, *Journal of Marketing*, 31 (4), 22–27.

Harter, Susan (2002), Authenticity, in *Handbook of Positive Psychology*, Charles Richard Snyder and Shane J. López, eds., New York: Oxford University Press, 382–394.

Higgins, E. Tory (1987), Self-Discrepancy: A Theory Relating Self and Affect, *Psychological Review*, 94 (3), 319–40.

Howe, Neil and William Strauss (2000), *Millenials Rising: The Next Great Generation*, New York: Vintage Books.

Kent, Robert J. and Chris T. Allen (1994), Competitive Interference Effects in Consumer Memory for Advertising: The Role of Brand Familiarity, *Journal of Marketing,* 58 (July), 97–105.

Lecky, Prescott (1945), *Self-Consistency: A Theory of Personality*, New York: Island Press.

Lenhart, Amanda, Kristen Purcell, Aaron Smith, and Kathryn Zickuhr (2010), *Social Media and Mobile Internet Use Among Teens and Young Adults*, retrieved on July 9, 2011 from http://www.pewinternet.org/Reports/2010/Social-Media-and-Young-Adults.aspx.

Malär, Lucia, Harley Krohmer, Wayne D. Hoyer, and Bettina Nyffenegger (2011), Emotional Brand Attachment and Brand Personality: The Relative Importance of the Actual and Ideal Self, *Journal of Marketing,* 75 (July), 35–52.

Markus, Hazel and Elissa Wurf (1987), The Dynamic Self-Concept: A Social Psychological Perspective, *Annual Review of Psychology*, 38, 299–337.

Morf, Carolyn C. and Frederick Rhodewalt (2001), Unraveling the Paradoxes of Narcissism: A Dynamic Self-Regulatory Processing Model, *Psychological Inquiry*, 12, 177–196.

Nadkarni, Ashwini and Stefan G. Hofmann (2011), Why Do People Use Facebook?, *Personality and Individual Differences*, 52, 243–249.

Nunnally, Jum C., Jr. (1978), *Psychometric Theory*, New York: McGraw-Hill.

Park, C.W., Deborah J. MacInnis, Joseph R. Priester, Andreas B. Eisingerich, and Dawn Iacobucci (2010), Brand Attachment and Brand Attitude Strength: Conceptual and Empirical Differentiation of two Critical Brand Equity Drivers, *Journal of Marketing*, 74 (6), 1–17.

Raskin, Robert N. and Calvin S. Hall (1979), A Narcissistic Personality Inventory, *Psychological Reports*, 45, 590.

Raskin, Robert N. and Calvin S. Hall (1981), The Narcissistic Personality Inventory: Alternate from Reliability and Further Evidence of Construct Validity, *Journal of Personality Assessment*, 45, 159–162.

Raskin, Robert N. and Howard Terry (1988), A Principle Component Analysis of the Narcissistic Personality Inventory and Further Evidence of its Construct Validity, *Journal of Personality and Social Psychology*, 56, 393–404.

Rhodewalt, Frederick and Carolyn C. Morf (1995), Self and Interpersonal Correlates of the Narcissistic Personality Inventory, *Journal of Research in Personality*, 29, 1–23.

Sedikides, Constantine, Aiden P. Gregg, Sylwia Cisek, and Claire M. Hart (2007), The I That Buys: Narcissists as Consumers, *Journal of Consumer Psychology*, 17, 254–257.

Sedikides, Constantine and Michael J. Strube (1997), Self-Evaluation: To Thine Own Self be Good, to Thine Own Self Be Sure, To Thine Own Self Be True, and To Thine Own Self Be Better, in *Advances in Experimental Social Psychology*, M.P. Zanna, ed. San Diego: Academic Press, 29, 209–269.

Sirgy, Michael J. (1982), Self-Concept in Consumer Behavior: A Critical Review, *Journal of Consumer Research*, 9 (3), 287–300.

Sirgy, M. Joseph, Dhruv Grewal, Tamara F. Mangleburg, Jae-ok Park, Kye-Sung Chon, C. B. Claiborne, J. S. Johar, and Harold Berkman (1997), Assessing the Predictive Validity of Two Methods of Measuring Self-image Congruence, *Journal of the Academy of Marketing Science*, 25 (3), 229–241.

Swann, William B., Jr. (1983), Self-Verification: Bringing Social Reality into Harmony with the Self, in *Greenwald Social Psychological Perspectives on the Self*, J. Suls and G. Anthony, eds. Hillsdale: Lawrence Erlbaum Associates, 33–66.

Swann, William B., Jr. and Stephen J. Read (1980), Self-Verification Processes: How We Sustain Our Self-Conceptions, *Journal of Experimental Social Psychology,* 17 (4), 351-372.

Tian, Kelly Tepper, William O. Bearden, and Gary L. Hunter (2001), Consumers' Need for Uniqueness: Scale Development and Validation, *Journal of Consumer Research,* 28 (1), 50–66.

Thomson, Matthew, Deborah J. MacInnis, and C. Whan Park (2005), The Ties That Bind: Measuring the Strength of Consumers' Emotional Attachments to Brands, *Journal of Consumer Psychology,* 15 (1), 77–91.

Trzesniewski, Kali H., M. Brent Donnellan, and Richard W. Robins (2008), Do Today's Young People Really Think They Are so Extraordinary? An Examination of Secular Changes in Narcissism and Self-Enhancement, *Psychological Science*, 19, 181–188.

Twenge, Jean M. (2006), Generation Me: Why Today's Young Americans Are More Confident, Assertive, Entitled—and More Miserable Than Ever Before, New York: Free Press.

Twenge, Jean M. and W. Keith Campbell (2009), *Living in The Age of Entitlement: The Narcissism Epidemic*, New York: Free Press.

Twenge, Jean M., Sara Konrath, Joshua D. Foster, W. Keith Campbell, and Brad J. Bushman (2008), Further Evidence of An Increase in Narcissism Among College Students, *Journal of Personality, 76* (4), 919-928.

Vazire, Samine and David C. Funder (2006), Impulsivity and The Self-Defeating Behavior of Narcissists, *Personality and Social Psychology Review*, 10, 154–165.

Vazire, Simine, Laura P. Naumann, Peter J. Rentfrow, and Samuel D. Gosling (2008), Portrait of a Narcissist: Manifestations of Narcissism in Physical Appearance, *Journal of Research in Personality*, 42, 1439–1447.

Wylie, Ruth C. (1979), *The Self-Concept: Theory and Research on Selected Topics* (Vol. 2), Lincoln: University of Nebraska Press.